Be Ye Transformed By The Renewal Of Your Mind

Calvin Thompson

Copyright © 2015 for Calvin Thompson

All rights reserved. No part of this publication may be reproduced, distributed, or transmitted in any form or by any means, including photocopying, recording, or other electronic or mechanical methods, without the prior written permission of the publisher, except in the case of brief quotations embodied in critical reviews and certain other noncommercial uses permitted by copyright law. For permission requests, write to the publisher, addressed "Attention: Permissions Coordinator," at the address below.

Scriblical Vibez Publishing, LLC
P. O. Box 6215
Plymouth, MI 48170-6215
www.scriblicalvibez.com

Ordering Information:

Quantity sales. Special discounts are available on quantity purchases by corporations, associations, and others. For details, contact the publisher at the address above.

Printed in the United States of America.

Dedication

I dedicate this book to my parents William and Eula Thompson; although they are not present in the physical sense, their memory is etched in my consciousness, and I am always aware of their presence. They kept a close watch over me in my formative years. At times, I felt like they were overprotective and smothered me, but I know their goal was to keep me on the straight and narrow path in the eyesight of God.

They prayed for me in my times of distress, and they praised me and gave me strength in my resolve to keep the faith. The lessons that they taught me I have passed on to my children and my children's children. I am who I am in large measure because of who they were, common folk of uncommon valor. People of humble beginnings but knew the intricate nature of things. They understood the simplicity of things about the profound implications of life. They knew the Lord and wanted their children to develop a personal relationship with him as well. I thank you both for all that you did and all that you aspired to achieve.

It's Our Time

Table of Contents

Dedication iii

Acknowledgments vii

Prologue ix

Introduction xi
   It's Our Time to Stop Procrastinating xiii

It's Our Time 1
   How I Feel 5
   Giving Thanks 9
   Encouragement 12
   All of God's Days Are Good 16
   Love 18
   Loving with a Renewed Mind 21
   When a Man Finds a Wife, He Finds a Good Thing 24
   Don't Give Up 30
   Change 36
   Remember to Remember 40
   Daddy's Little Girls 42

Letters to the Constellation 51
   Dear Antoine 55
   Dear Antoine 59
   My Dad's Birthday 64
   A Letter to My Brother 67
   Dear Nip 69
   Dear Wesley 72
   Dear Antoine 75

The Transformation 81
    Manifesting My Desires 85
    Leaving 90
    Church Life 98
    Manifestation 101
    Be Not Conformed to the World 105

Transformation 109
    We Are Transformed by the Renewal of Our Mind 112
    Living My Life Like It's Golden 115
    What Is Going On in 2010? 117
    Reconciliation 122
    Letting Go and Letting God 126
    Spiritual Integrity 129
    Spiritual Integration 131
    Think About What You Think About 133
    We Are Transformed by the Renewal of Our Mind 135
    A New Creature in Christ 136
    Perseverance 138
    Dear Joshua 143
    Abundant Grace 148
    Gratitude 151
    Forgiveness 154
    It's My Time 157
    Afterthoughts 165
    Epilogue: Generational Conflict 168

Acknowledgments

I must make mention of my extended family. Coming from the era that I did when a neighborhood was a neighborhood, and everyone had a vested interest in seeing you do well, it was a village mentality. The elders of the village, who have gone on to glory, offered a timeless message as well. Shout out to the Hecla St. Alumni whose reach exceeded their grasp when it came to keeping the neighborhood children on point.

Worth noting is the spiritual connection that was formulated in a large part because of my affiliation with the Universal Triumph the Dominion of God under the leadership of the Shaffers and the entire Dominion family.

My dear brother Abdul, your prayers and thoughts were not in vain as well; thanks for supporting us in your relentless and persistent fashion. Nettie, I thank God for allowing you to be a part of my life.

Katrina and Tanya, you are at the top of my list. Well, you can say that I raised you, but in the reality of things, both of you raised me and continue to raise me, for you define me on so many levels.

Lela and the boys, I thank God for the experiences that he has allowed us to have. For that, I am forever grateful. Rest assure, this is not as good as it gets; the best is yet to come if you only believe.

Someone who has displayed the epitome of friendship, as the Bible states a true friend is like a brother, is my spiritual brother Gary. We made this journey together. Thank you for everything.

Angel, your name says it all. You truly are a source of inspiration and delight.

Prologue

In our attempt to make sense of our existence, mankind has always considered those things which are external to him. But now it is time to get acquainted with that which is inside of him. To become aware of that indwelling spirit that dwells inside of him. Yes, I use Christianity and themes thereof not because it is the only model to consider. But I say that there are eternal truths that are present within Christianity that have practical implications.

When reference is made to "let this mind be in you that was also in Christ Jesus," this has profound implications consistent with the fact that Jesus personalized his relationship with God and so can we. We must be mindful that Jesus was the prototype of what we can be and that we all are privy to the Christ potential.

My quest is to understand the practical side of your spiritual walk. That you can be one with God and that it is not some abstract notion removed from you that it can be an integral part of your being if you only believe. To know what it means to have a personal relationship with God is our reality. and we should furnish the life so that God can use us. It is a matter of making the right choices, and once we know better, we can do better.

We can have our heaven right here on this earth, and if we live right, heaven belongs to us. Heaven is a state of mind and the mindset that we are willing to entertain, so how we choose to think is an important matter. We must have an open mind and be willing to reinvent ourselves. Be mindful of this fact: we are innovators and creators by nature. It was not the Creator's intentions that we should be passive in our walk.

God intends for us to have a full and abundant life, and we do suffer needlessly by operating outside of the will of God. If we really understood how dynamic we are and lived accordingly, we could move mountains. We are stifled by our fears and doubts because we lend ourselves to a way of thinking that is inconsistent with our nature. We must lend ourselves to an elevated posture and accept the fact that we can do all things through Christ who strengthens us.

It is our time to accept that it is possible to live a spirit-filled existence and that "we can get along" if we choose to. It is our choice and decision making that either makes us or breaks us. We can blame others for our predicament, but just as the problems began with us, so does the solution. We must take responsibility for our needs and resolve our issues.

Introduction

"Nobody told me the road would be easy, but God did not bring me this far to leave me alone."

This is my contribution to society, something that I longed to do for years. An accumulation of information from a variety of sources intended to assist you on your journey. Some information is from the written word, and just as valuable, in the oral tradition handed down from people who understood life and had the wisdom bestowed upon them from God.

Our God is an awesome God, and we all can achieve extraordinary things if we only believe and trust in the essential ingredient that we come from. The creator has a plan for us all. I am mindful of a passage in the Holy Quran that states that God revealed himself to all the people throughout the land. Therefore, there is no one who can say they did not have a chance to be redeemed.

For God loves us all, and he has blessings for us. All we must do is reach up and get it. One must focus on elevating always and know that deliverance is near. We should humble ourselves, and the Lord will draw nearer to us. There are challenges in our life, but we must look to God for guidance and know for a surety that God is our inexhaustible vein of supply and that whatever we need God has it.

I did not always know the Lord, but I take solace in the fact that he knew me. There were many challenges that I had in life. I became a prayerful person in my later years. Silly me, a dear friend once told me that I should pray to God and ask him for guidance. I didn't know any better.

I said I didn't want to burden God with my problems. But as time went on, I realized, like my father once said, I took my problems to the altar, and when I felt better, I took them back. But I learned the value of leaving my problems at the altar and letting the Lord work them out.

Well, we live, and we learn, and I learned there is no failure with God. I tried it my way, and my best thinking created the mess that I was in. Now I know the value of not being conformed to the world, and that we are the embodiment of the word.

In my writings, there is repetitive dialogue, and it may appear to be overkill. But in the realities of our existence, we are inundated with toxic dialogue that puts us in dire straits. It is often alluded to that if you hear the falsehoods over and over, they become the truth. With that in mind, in the same manner, we must hear the truth repeatedly until it becomes acceptable as a possibility.

Although we are in the human realm, we must remember that our religion should not be some abstract notion removed from us. To the contrary, it should be something tangible and pragmatic that we can achieve and demonstrate in our daily walk. It should be a way of life, not something that we achieve after we die. We should and can be transformed while we yet have life in our body.

It's Our Time to Stop Procrastinating

If you at least just step out on faith and start working toward building a better relationship with God, God will do the rest. When you finally get yourself to the point where you want to do better, you stand at the threshold of a transformation that you must be prepared to see through. It is comparable to the adage a thousand-mile journey began with that single step in that direction.

I thought about authoring a book for years before I initiated it. Over a period, I just began to write a series of compositions just based on my experiences and my feelings related to those events. One theme led to other themes, and the next thing you know, those thoughts did become things. It was if the writings took on a life of their own, and I just became a willing participant. So, it is validity in just taking the initiative, and God will do the rest. We, essentially, need to trust in the process. The law of attraction states that you attract those things that you desire to have. Conjoined with that is that you attract to you that which you are.

In consideration of that, now that I had started drafting my book, it was time to bring this assignment to completion. It truly has been an odyssey, and true to form to say the least. I realize that I have grown immensely through the process of gathering my thoughts and experiences while working to complete this book. Throughout the years, I have learned that it is not the destination alone that defines you, but how you apply what you learn from the journey that makes the greatest impact on your life. I've discovered that this entire process has been a form of catharsis for me, which has been the catalyst to help me grow into the person that I aspired to become.

Recently, I started looking over my life and saw that my transformation and renewing of my mind began long before I decided to write this book. Maybe it was a result of resilience or the fact that I was too afraid to repeat cycles that I knew were against who God created me to be. I decided that being consumed with fear and doubt did not have to dictate my life.

Relying on others to validate my vision of me doesn't have to hinder or define me either. There are still things to contend with, but those are things that I am willing to address. They are an inconvenience, and that is okay. Part of your personal growth and development would challenge you to deal with your fears and doubts. When pursuing your dreams, it's important to look at the rewards ... *and* the cost involved. It is something to be said about *nothing ventured nothing gained.*

I wouldn't be the person that I am had it not been for taking the risks to achieve my objectives. Against the wishes of others, I became a father at 18. That was not my plans. But I made a conscious effort to do just that; I could have done differently and pursued my own agenda. When my daughters told me, years later, how grateful they were that I didn't abandon them like so many fathers of that era did, I realized I needed to hear that form them. In addition to becoming a young father, before I was 25, I had experienced two nervous breakdowns, and I found myself so challenged by my own issues, but I was determined to make it. With the demands of everything and my determination to make it, I experienced my own wandering in the wilderness episode. I started college with a baby on the way, and by the time I finished college, I had a grandbaby on the way.

In the meantime, after love appeared to be so evasive, I did get married at 36. Interesting for me, I married at a time when I was leaning toward putting that energy into my career. I chose to be married. Being married was something I always felt compelled to do. Even though it had eluded, I still desired it. It took the intervention of a significant mother figure (Mother Woods) in my life to tell me that marriage was eminent for me. To get other things out of the way and get myself prepared for matrimony, I took what Mother Woods predicted to heart. Before she completed her sentence, things began to materialize. My wife would soon appear. I had met my wife months before we started dating, and when I saw her again (she was a friend of my niece), things just evolved in a manner like it was just meant to be. Even my father had suggested to me that I should marry and have more children. It was like the universe was reconfiguring my life because I did marry, and I did have more children.

Regardless of what your plans are and what unfolds in your life, God has a plan for us all. We are fortunate if we understand and follow the plan that God has for our life. For during all the challenges that I have had to contend with, God brought me through it all. I have been fortunate with the trials and tribulations that I had to contend with that I never lost my joy for life.

The presence of the Lord in my life, even when I didn't have a clue, was apparent when I reflected and looked over my life and experiences. God had been and continues to be a comforting factor in my life. He has carried me through the tumultuous relationships that I have had with myself, for the battle has been in my mind.

The most important component of our being is our mind—as it is said that as a man thinks and believes in his heart so is he. The biggest challenge that I have always had to contend with were the manner and methods of my thinking. For everything is predicated on how one thinks, for you can think yourself into success or failure. It's why I chose the theme (and title) for my book: *Be Ye Transformed by The Renewal of Your Mind*. An interesting concept that I have been exposed to is that we are to be mindful of the way and manner we think. For our thoughts are things, and words do materialize. Even in the realm of psychology, we were taught that it is our predominate thoughts that influence our actions the most. Essentially our thoughts are self-fulfilling or prophetic by nature.

Be mindful of the thoughts that you attend to. If there are any thoughts that come into your mind that our contrary to the will of the creator, don't entertain them. Everything is preceded by a thought. Even in psychiatry, the precipitate before the onset of the disease is always attended to. Nothing just occurs; there must be precipitating factors. Mind your mind, think about what you think about as the late Dr. Lorraine Kiefer Witherspoon stated. One cannot underestimate the thought/action connection. For years, I subscribed to the wrong notion of myself. Consumed with doubt and fear, not fully understanding that I was perpetuating my limitations. I was causing an incongruence, formulating a plan but negating it by not trusting in the process, being hearers of the word, but not being doers of the word. It wasn't until I began to see it and believing that what I expounded for others could be for myself as well that I finally understand.

I like to use the illustrations that my brand strategist Yahminah McIntosh stated—that I had been hiding behind a veil and that these qualities had not been nurtured within me. When she said that, it was like a confirmation as well as a clarification of something that I had always considered. Giving someone reassurance and support is something that in my vocation that I always extended to others. It is when you are on the receiving end of the process that you see how valuable of an exchange it is.

Now at this juncture in my life, I must see myself as actualizing those things that I desire to achieve. Embracing the process instead of avoiding it. It is like now that this is my reality, there is no turning back because I have a renewed mindset. Fear and doubt, that part of Calvin is no longer the definitive part of me. While it is an attribute that I have, it is not the only thing that defines me. Now, it is my time, and I can pursue those things that as I reflect on had eluded me. For the Lord will elevate you in accordance with your faith, and he can do no more for you than he can through you. Accepting something as an accomplished fact is a key element in renewing your mind. Just as Jesus said the Father and I are one. We must go beyond the self-imposed constraints that we impose upon ourselves.

Yes, we see athletes and entertainers accomplishing their dreams. We say that God is no respecter of persons; what he has done for others he will do for us in the biblical sense. But it is what we do to let that be our reality that matters for us. For that, I had to address and go public with my challenges with mental health concerns—as well as how that has and does impact on my life, even today. But like I was told that in telling my story it no longer belongs to me;

it belongs to the universe. I can see that now. My story and my life unfolded just like it was decreed to occur. There were certain parts of it that I did not understand at its inception, but over time, the reasons and reasoning became quite clear.

After an extended period of working in mental health, I understand the intricacies of the mind and psychic in ways that I would have never considered. When I first started working in psychiatry, I thought it would be for a short time because I had other ambitions of pursuing a career in law. But the more I worked in psychiatry, the more fascinated I became. It's like I was called to do this. My experiences are what propelled me into the role.

Along the way, I felt a calling to be a minister; that within itself has been my most rewarding venture. Either way with psychiatry or the ministry, you are dealing with the mind. For me, the two complement one another.

At this juncture, I can sincerely say that everything is in divine order. On reflection, God did a marvelous job in revealing himself through me and for me. I accomplished so much on my journey. What God has for you is for you. In writing my book, a pattern began to emerge; it is not just what happened to me but how I chose to deal with it. Even amid the storm or adversities, it was my perception of things that mattered the most. I must take a fearless inventory of myself.

At the end of the day, it is how I chose to deal with myself and others. A theme that my wife would always reiterate to me is that between being in the ministry, working in psychiatry, and being a teacher, I had to find a way to deal with my children better. Often, one can have more objectivity in their dealings with others than what it is up close and personal with your loved ones. That is awkward and contrary to the way that things need to be, but it is

INTRODUCTION — *IT'S OUR TIME TO STOP PROCRASTINATING*

a fact. Again, one of the critical components of witting is that you get an opportunity to convey and express things that need to be expressed. Writing is s phenomenal tool of expression; it is like I can get into a character that I need to be, to express a part of myself that needs to be expressed through me.

Prior to the prospects of publishing my writings, it was through the encouragement of others that I began to consider becoming an author as a possibility. I really was on a quest to go to another level of awareness. I was on a mission to explore new frontiers within myself. People were impressed with what I said, but they wanted to know more about Calvin. It was a time to go beyond the limitations of fear.

Little did I know that my journey would take me to new heights and the manifestation of my desires. En route, my path would afford me the opportunity to meet people who helped me achieve the next rung in the ladder to remind me that God would allow me to achieve things that I desired if I only believed and trusted in the process, for there is a part of me that will confront my fears despite being afraid. And with this knowledge, I understood that in confronting fears I can extend myself beyond my grasp.

People who lead by example who has achieved that which you desire to achieve, they have their challenges to contend with but have excelled anyway, and they are the first to admit that their journey hasn't been easy, but that it did get better because they got out of the way and let the process work.

We are often encouraged to be that light that we want to see and to lead by example. I have lived a faith-based existence, and that has served me well. I like to say that I have been inspired by my experiences and became the person that I am because of them. I can be remorseful and say why me. But all things considered, I must say that I have prevailed because that was my path, and I was put here to master my impediments.

Going public with mental health challenges is something so different than what I am accustomed to doing. Because I have spent a lifetime not disclosing it because of the fear of reprisal and scrutiny of others. This journey started 40 years ago as a young adult with the weight of the world on my shoulders, not knowing what to do or how to do things, inexperienced with life and growing into a role that was altogether different than the life I had planned for myself.

It would take me years to understand my role, but in time, it did clarify itself. That is the blessing in disguise. It took everything that I went through to become the person that I am. All the grief and despair as well as the prayers of my mother and father. Amid the insecurities and self-doubt over time, I transformed into the person that I am.

There is greatness inside all of us. In my case, I was afforded an opportunity to go from such a low point in life, feeling so bad about myself and circumstances, to a point of not just being encouraged by others but to a point of encouraging others. The Lord raised me up to the stature that I am, and I must give him the glory, for he allowed the doctors to have the knowledge to help me on my journey. So, I am indebted to both the medical community as well as to God. So, in writing my book, I am mindful of the adage *to much is given much is expected*. For the Lord has blessed me to be a blessing to others. The transformation that occurs is consistent with the construct that problems cannot be solved at the same level of thinking that created them. I have been afforded the opportunity to go beyond the constraints of societal definitions as well as self-imposed constraints of myself. The Lord allowed me to go through a transformation and reach the heights that I have achieved.

INTRODUCTION — *IT'S OUR TIME TO STOP PROCRASTINATING*

The reference point for me is that not only have I worked in the field of mental health services, but I have been the recipient of mental health services for the past forty years. I was motivated to work in mental health in large part because I recognized a need to help others. I had an experience of being hospitalized at Northville State Hospital. This was not my first hospitalization, but it was my last. When I was first hospitalized, like a lot of people, I was resistant to the process. I was on track to achieve so much more, and being a patient wasn't on my agenda. I was in college with the intentions of going to law school. Additionally, I had started a family the summer before I started college.

Adjusting to college was difficult enough by itself—added to that was the obligation of a family. I was young and naïve to the ways of the world, not understanding myself and carrying the weight of the world on my shoulders. It was a time when I was still dependent on my parents for both financial and emotional support and needed guidance and reassurance, and at some point, I didn't know how to articulate my needs to others or to myself. Things became difficult when I began to become not just estranged from others but from myself as well. Some of the decisions that I made became a recipe for disaster.

A pivotal time for me occurred when I became estranged from my father, and we stopped communicating. I needed him, but we had a disagreement, and I shut down all communication with him, which essentially, had me like a ship without a rudder, treading in treacherous waters and sinking at the same time. The more I struggled, the more difficult my life became. The events that would make my life go from bad to worst consumed me with grief and despair that would cause me to make decisions that would have dire complications for me. Several months after dealing with the challenges that I had with my baby mama drama, I began to feel even more overwhelmed. I started trying to please everyone else and neglected myself, which ultimately affected my decision making. I truly believe that it was the combination of everything that I was going through that caused my first breakdown. There was a lot going on and so many things that I felt that I needed to do in order to make my life have purpose again. I started working to make amends to show everyone that I could fix a relationship with my daughters' mother and repair the damage to the relationship with my parents. I felt like I had let everyone down and was not living up to the expectations of others.

I felt that my deliverance had come in securing a job in an automobile plant. Well, that changed almost as quick as I started working there. I had a verbal altercation with a foreman, and he threatened to fire me. I was so distraught, and my spirits were crushed. But I later learned that my father wanted me to quit then and there. Shortly after that, I was transferred to another department that would ultimately be the end of my tenure.

I was on a collision course when I look back on it—trying to be a full-time student while working in an automobile plant and dealing with a family. Once again, because of what I put myself through, people did want me to quit. The change in the department did not mean that my situation would improve.

The change in departments also meant that I was in a situation where I'd be expected to work 12-hour shifts. At this point, with my determination to make it, I was going through a mountainous situation with a mindset that was unrealistic with a goal that was not achievable.

My daily grind would be to work 12 hours then go to school in the evening. I would awaken at one in the morning and then go to bed at ten that night. This went on for an extended period. I was determined to make 90 days, and I did, but it was at this point that I experienced an emotional breakdown. For me, 90 days was my objective to achieve seniority, and then things would get better.

That was both the mindset and the physical grind that I extended myself to. When George Foreman, years later after his defeat by Muhammad Ali, was asked what he would have done differently, he said he would have stayed off the ropes. I understand his response; looking back, I would have stayed off the ropes or considered other options. My mother asked me if I knew that I could have talked to someone. Even my brother Wesley stated that my parents wanted me to quit the job or the schooling. But that is one of the challenges that we must resolve—how we deal with someone when they are on a collision course. Someone has to be receptive to intervention or deliverance from themselves. Even with the best advice, the recipient must take it. Everything is centered around the mindset or the thoughts that we engage in.

We are creatures of habit. It is our predominate thoughts that we engage in that have the most influence over our behavior. Be mindful of the thoughts that we entertain and the thoughts that we give authority over the situation. For as a man thinks and believes in his heart, so is he. Our thoughts and feelings and emotions are one. In the transformation process, because it is a process, we must be mindful of the thoughts we entertain because we all are creatures of habit, and we can give justification to anything that we do. It's why we are encouraged in the spiritual realm to lean more on the Lord and not our own understanding. Look to God for guidance always, and trust in the process. Otherwise, we can operate in a manner that is outside of the will of God, a mindset that fosters a relationship that is not conducive to our wellbeing.

We can give credence to anything that we do, and it can happen to anyone at any time. When I reflect on the time when my life was falling apart and contrast it to where I am now, one thing I realize is that I don't need to compare. Who I was then is exactly that—who I was *then*. That's the beauty of life; you can change. I have become the person that I am because of the events that influenced me then. I have had so many challenges in my life since then. But the mindset that governs my behavior is so different, and my behavior reflects those levels of awareness of the awesome force that resides within me. I aspire to do so much with my life. I have had a phenomenal life because of my experiences. When I think about where I am despite the mountainous challenges that I must contend with. Even when I didn't know what and how things were going to go for me. The Lord made my crooked path straight. He allowed me to go through something just to get to the other side. This book, which is part autobiography and a part inspirational, is *my* story. But is also *your* story because we all have a story, and we all go through challenges in our lives. It takes some people years to get up the nerve to tell their stories, and there are others who go to their graves with their stories never told. After all that I have learned in my life and what I believe God has done in my life, I did not want to procrastinate any more. It is often stated that there is no testimony without a test. When God does something for you, enabling you to make it through a major challenge, you should shout it from the rooftop. I realized that this book is my roof top and the more I share, the louder my shout becomes.

It's Our Time

To go beyond the limitations that we have imposed upon ourselves—that should be our quest. Will it be easy? No, but it is a part of our reinvention or continuous improvement. Somethings are an essential ingredient in our life as we evolve in our understanding of not just who we are but who we can be.

Yes, I said it, there is more to our life than having a 9 to 5. A vacation in the summer or in the winter if we are fortunate to do so. This is defining ourselves in such narrow terms. This does address our material side of life. But shouldn't we go beneath the surface and embrace other core values? Our material attributes do make us comfortable, and monies are a requirement in a material world.

We must look at the big picture and assess the needs of the whole person, and that is what this book is all about, for you to recognize that you can have a full and abundant life and to aid you in obtaining it.

Beyond that, it's also about getting your mind uncluttered and removing the shackles that keep you consumed with fears and doubt, stifling you and causing you not to pursue your dreams and aspirations. To go forward, you must identify those things that you allow to get in the way of actualizing your vision of yourself. To confront yourself on yourself, be willing to do fearless inventory of yourself and to be okay with it.

We have so much going on in our head and heart, it becomes difficult to figure out what came first the chicken or the egg. Well, not to oversimplify the process, it is the idea or thought that precedes the action that we must be mindful of.

For thoughts are things, and words do materialize. We can impact our life and the lives of others. As a matter of fact, we do, it's just that we have until now left it up to chance. Now, we must be more concerted in how we do things, to be more proactive instead of reactive.

It is an interesting time to be on this planet at this critical time because we are going through a paradigm shift, a shift in the way that we think as well how we deal with things and one another. The customary practices and rules of engagement are not serving us well. We really have fallen, and we must get up. We have been wandering in the wilderness for too long. We are at critical mass, and we must do something about it. The solution resides within you.

In the aggregate, we are all responsible for the mess that we are in. With that in mind, the problems that we have created also have to be resolved by us. We must get on a better accord with one another and start using our resources to improve our lot with the understanding that we can; it is a matter of the choices that we make. As it is written, we are suffering needlessly, and we are perishing because of a lack of knowledge. That knowledge resides in this fact—that we really must realize how dynamic we are and can be.

We need to be reintroduced to who we really are and what we really can be. Our awareness goes beyond the traditional assumptions of both religiosity and traditional assumptions of psychology. It is important that we become more mindful of the thoughts that we entertain and that there is power in the words that we use.

We cannot continue to look for something to fall out of the sky and save us; we must do the work. It is just not enough to look for someone else to save us; we must save ourselves. This is not just a job for one person, everyone must have an active role in their salvation. We cannot be passive in our walk; we must trust in the process of awakening the sleeping giant that resides within us.

Just like we have inherited the mess within us, we have also inherited the solution. Again, the power is in the way that we think. We must shift gears and magnify our faith and our resolve to change our condition. People often talk about Jesus and what he did; Jesus also states we have the same potential to be Christ like that he did. He was our model of excellence.

Grow beyond the self-imposed limitations that we have imposed upon ourselves. There is greatness inside of us yearning to express itself; we just must trust in the process. These attributes of excellence must be nurtured and cultivated.

Never mind the flight to Mars—we should put more emphasis on the internal exploration and what you can conceive of that is possible within you. Go inwardly to the inner recesses of your mind. Read a book or write a book. Empower yourself. Dare to dream again. Soar like an eagle. Run like a gazelle and begin to believe in yourself again. You don't know what you can do until you try.

No matter how great the accomplishment of others has been, everyone had to start at the beginning. Give yourself a chance every day. You have an opportunity to reinvent yourself. It's all relevant;

we can achieve what we desire to the best of our ability. This is not as good as it gets. No, the best is yet to come if you only believe. Let's get started and do what we can. What we can't do we will rely on our God to do.

How I Feel

At this moment, I am experiencing a variety of feelings. The first thing that comes to mind is that I'm repeating the same mantra at the end of this year that I did the year before. : "I have to do something better." Now what that "better" translates into has yet to be determined. I often view myself as someone who authors the next great book or produces the next best speech. As I said, the medium or modality is yet to be determined. But I like to think of myself as a work in progress. As I often affirm, this is not as good as it gets. To the contrary, I often tell myself the best is yet to come.

So many people told me that there was a book buried inside of me, but I just took it as normal encouragement and kept going. The truth is, I never saw myself getting to this point and actually being able to finish a book. Once I challenged myself to stop procrastinating and started working on this book, there was no turning back. I often tell others to pursue their dreams or to tap into their creativity, yet still I continue to defer my own. In the beginning, I stifled my own creativity and stunted my own growth, which led me here ... to a new beginning. Nowhere is it written that one could achieve their objective without putting forward the effort. Biblically speaking: "faith without works is dead." One must put forth the effort to make something tangible, and it all begins in the conceptual mode.

We all have qualities that exist deep within us or in what some may call the idealized mode of existence, but for it to materialize, one must put forth the work. As the verbiage of today states: "don't talk about it, be about it." Great ideas come and go, but the ones that materialize reflect the author's faith and burning desire to see them manifest. As in my case, there is a certain level of doubt and fear that I am working hard to relinquish for my dreams to manifest.

As my friend and confidante informed me, don't look for others to validate you; go inwardly to look for answers. Even more poignant and concise, my beloved minister informed me to rise above the human eclipsiation.

I believe it's necessary to learn how to see myself without being so critical of who I am and what I do. It wasn't until I decided to stop questioning my ability to be delivered from myself and doubting the godliness that resides inside of me that I started working on this project. We often make our plight bigger than our God, something I can attest to that I have worked to be delivered from. It was my own insecurities and sense of inadequacies that plagued me for too long and prevented me from rising to the heights that God has already decreed for me. This is how I feel, and this is my truth.

As I encouraged others to do some soul searching and go inwardly to find themselves, it is time for the teacher to become a student again and to partake of his own advice. Jesus said it best—we must be one with God and let his will be done. To trust more on the Holy Spirit to guide and direct our path. Once we allow God's will to guide and direct our path, we come into a greater awareness of what our true purpose in life is.

Be mindful that we are made in God's image and likeness. God breathed into the nostrils of man and made him a living soul. The word "breath" and the word "spirit" have the same root meaning, so God's spirit resides within us. Therefore, it is only natural that we should be on one accord with God naturally speaking; we should not be separate from God at any time or point in our life.

We are God's manifestation and expression here on earth. We are spirits housed in a body. When my minister informs us to rise above the human eclipsiation, it encourages us to recognize that our spirituality exceeds our human traits. It would seem at times we allow our humanness to exceed our spirituality, which becomes evident in how we allow our problems to be bigger than our God. As it has been stated: "If you pray, why worry, and if you worry, why pray?"

Being consumed with fear and doubt and allowing these things to take root in our mind is the source of our grief and confusion. But it is at this point that it's important to remind us that God is not the author of confusion. To the contrary, it is incumbent upon us that anything that is contrary to God's commandments should not take root in our mind. Think about a letter that comes to your house that is not yours. You promptly return that letter to the sender. Such is the case with thoughts that enter your mind that are incompatible with your spiritual nature; you send them back into the universe. Don't let these thoughts that compromise your spiritual integrity take root in your consciousness.

The apostle Paul stated that he died daily. He was referring to the carnality and the sinful existence that one could have. He also stated for us not to be conformed to this world but be transformed by the renewal of our mind. The thoughts we entertain are so profound, and as such, they have a self-fulfilling prophecy to them. As the Bible states, "as a man thinks so is he." Thoughts are things, and words materialize. Having a mind made up to serve the Lord is so important.

Renouncing anything that is contrary to God's will is important as the Bible states we are to keep God's commandments and live. If you live right, heaven belongs to you. Heaven is described as a peaceful state of mind.

As the Bible states, let this mind be in you that is also in Christ Jesus, and Christ is a consciousness that resides in all of mankind. Jesus recognized and realized his Christ potential and so should we. He became one with God and let the process work. He submitted to God's will unabated, and the rest is history.

Giving Thanks

First and foremost, I must give thanks to almighty God for finding favor in me and for allowing me to have the amazing journey we call life. Truly he has been a watchman on the wall and added surety to my path every step of the way. The finest and most sophisticated GPS system pales in comparison to the ease of which the Lord has made my journey. Any potential obstacle was either averted or dealt with as he saw fit. Either I climbed over the mountain, or the mountain was moved as the good Lord decreed the matter.

Oh, what a mighty God we serve that neither sleeps or slumbers, that gives us ample warning and guidance in all matters and reminds us of the eternal benefits of keeping his commandments and living a full and abundant life. Lest we forget, the Bible is a resource for us to look to for guidance. We are instructed to look at the Lord's faithful servant Job, a man with spiritual integrity who remained steadfast in his convictions while facing mountainous obstacles.

We must be mindful that Job is the prototype of the enormous potential that we have in the divine mind of Christ. As the Bible states, lean on the Lord and not your own understanding, and trust in the process.

We are made in the image and likeness of almighty God; as such, we are a form of God. In that core belief, we are the manifestation and expression of God here on earth. Again, the Bible states that we are not to be conformed to the world but to be transformed by the renewal of the mind.

We are the personification of God, fundamentally spirits housed in a body having the mind of God. Oftentimes, we think of ourselves as human beings having spiritual encounters. No, to the contrary, first and foremost we are spiritual beings having a human experience.

To achieve this objective, we must rise above the human eclipsiation and lean on the divine mind of Christ to live a Christ-centered existence. Christ is the mind of God individualized. Christ is the knowledge and wisdom of God unto salvation.

God knows the unlimited potential that resides within man. The amazing thing about Jesus is he wanted mankind to realize his divinity as well. As it is written, "great things have I done but greater things shall you do, let this mind be in you that was also in Christ Jesus." Jesus came to show us the divinity that resides within all of us. The gratitude that we display comes from living a life that will allow us to live in accordance to the will of God.

Jesus recognized the importance of being on one accord with God when he stated the "Father and I are one." The goal is to live a life leaning not to our own understanding but reaching for God's divine guidance. This is where our desire to be conformed to the world lessens and our desire to reach to be more like God becomes even greater.

We should recognize the omnipresence of God and recognize that wherever we are, God's presence should be known and felt. As we grow spiritually, our affairs should be in accordance to what is pleasing in the eyesight of God. When two or more are gathered in the name of the Lord, he is also in the midst. Do not exclude God from the equation or live a life that is contrary to his nature. We must remind ourselves that he created mankind in the best of molds with the best of intentions. He created you a little lower than the angels. As Jesus stated, we are to be busy going about doing God's business.

We should not allow ourselves to be put in compromising positions that would cause us to be separated from God. If there is any thought that we entertain that is contrary to the will of God, we should not let it take root in our consciousness.

Encouragement

When you step out on faith, and you travel the road less traveled, you must be willing to rise to the occasion and to remain steadfast in your convictions. It will not be easy, but this is an assignment that the Lord gave to you. You must do this irrespective to what the naysayers say and make turning your fear into faith your primary goal.

This is the burning desire that is part of the next dimension of your thinking; you are no longer a caterpillar. You are now a butterfly. You have been transformed. What is inside of you has emerged, and your destination is intertwined with the universe.

The remarkable thing about encouragement is that you need it whether you get it from others or not and like the Psalmist David stated: "if others don't encourage you then you have to encourage yourself."

In the same context, people around you may not understand what your particular needs are, but rest assure, that's a need you have to provide for yourself as well. Just because others may take you for granted doesn't mean you should take yourself for granted. Learn how to appreciate yourself and recognize the intrinsic value that you have irrespective to what is going on.

Be mindful of the awesome source that you come from because you're made in the image and likeness of almighty God, you are a form of God. When God made man, he had the noblest intentions. You are his manifestation and expression. Essentially, you are a spirit housed in a body.

Oftentimes, we become accustomed to think we are human beings with spiritual inclinations. No, to the contrary, our dominant trait is our spiritual essence. Be mindful of this fact and let this marinate in your consciousness.

Considering the source that we come from, we should live in accordance to the dictates or specifications of our Creator. As the Bible states, keep God's commandments and live. This process is likened to a manufacturer that creates a product accompanied by a list of specs to get the best usage out of the product. God embedded in our consciousness an awareness of how best to live and function or divine guidance.

Let this mind be in you that was also in Christ who being a form of God did not consider it robbery to be equal to God. It is imperative that we operate from a higher consciousness and to live accordingly. As you find more out about who you are in God, you will be inclined to not be live a life that is absent from the presence of God.

The thoughts that we entertain are so important. As the Bible states as a man thinks in his heart so is he. Thoughts become things; thoughts are things and words materialized. Start believing in your Christ potential and the unlimited capacity that you have in the mind of Christ.

Our God is awesome, and so are we, for he made us in the best of molds with the noblest intentions; we must honor our divinity. As it is written, we must furnish the life so that God can use us and follow his will irrespective to the circumstances.

We cannot ask God for something and not expect it; it's important to not waver in our faith but to make strengthening it our priority. I have come to realize with a surety that God is my inexhaustible vein of supply. This has been a year full of trials and tribulations, but through the grace of God, I have prevailed.

As David stated in Psalms: "I once was young, but now I am old. I have never seen the righteous forsaken or his seed go begging for bread." My gas was turned off four times during the period of my leap of faith. I was not even able to live in my house for a month. My family was scattered, and I was separated from my wife, but through it all God made a way out of no way.

Although a trial, this experience allowed me to be in the comfort of my brother's home where I was encouraged and exhorted. As a caregiver to countless others, I am so accustomed to giving reassurance and encouraging words to others, and during this period, I was the one who was asked if I was ok. When you are going through your own tribulations, you realize just how comforting those words are. I am eternally grateful to my brother and his family for welcoming me into their home and to God for allowing me to stand tall in the storm.

I am thankful to God for reminding me of his presence and that he had not forsaken me and that I will never walk alone. For God brought me through that mountainous situation, for as it is written, the battle is not yours; it is the Lord's. For God showed up and showed his might. When one is led by the Spirit of the Lord to go beyond the ordinary to the extraordinary, one must yield to the call.

God will see you through the transition and make your crooked path straight, for he knows the enormous potential that you have inside of you. He just wants you to become aware of the awesome qualities that you have inside of you as well.

Lean on the Lord and not your own understanding, and trust in the lord with all your might, and he will direct your path. God will put no more on us than what we can bear; he will make the way of escape for the faithful.

All of God's Days Are Good

Rev. Princess Maggie Shaffer often repeats the following statement: *All of God's days are good no matter what the prevailing conditions seem to be.* In the spiritual realm of our existence, she is right. God has blessings for us, and it is our responsibility to focus on elevation so that we may receive them. While in the midst of our journey, we should hold on to God's unchanging hands and maintain our spiritual integrity knowing that God will work it out for the faithful.

Eric Butterworth states in *Discover the Power within You*, "If you who believe in the divinity of man and the omnipresent of God but do not act as if you believe then what hope is there for the world." As they say, wherever I am, God is there. Be mindful of your duty to God always and operate as if you are in his presence as well. We should acknowledge God in all our endeavors and let him be the guiding force in our decision-making.

We suffer needlessly when we live a life contrary to the will of God. Whatever we need, God has it. No one told us that the road would be easy, but God did not bring us this far to leave us alone. Our assignment is to trust in that Divine Spirit to guide us with the full knowledge that God will never leave us alone.

There will be challenges that will seem insurmountable and mountainous by nature, but God will either remove it or give us the strength to climb. Remember, as it is written, we are made in the image and likeness of God. As such, we are a form of God. We are God's manifestation and expression here on earth. We are spirits housed in a body. We are not mere humans with spiritual inclinations. To the contrary, we are spiritual beings experiencing the human conditions.

We must come into an awareness of who we are in the eyesight of God. It is written, greater is he that is in you than that which is in the world. We are not to be conformed to the world but to be transformed by the renewal of our mind. In the ancient Sanskrit, "man" means "thinker." And as we know, what a man thinks in his heart so is he.

Our relationship with God is the key to our existence. As Jesus stated, the Father and I are one. Jesus was aware of his divinity and the source from which he came from and so should we. We have the very attributes of God inside of us. We are the personification of God; we have the Christ consciousness inside of us. Christ is the knowledge and wisdom of God unto salvation. Christ is the mind of God individualized. Coming into an awareness of being a child of God should be our quest.

To say that all of God's days are good is to acknowledge the omnipotence and the omnipresent of God and that wherever I am, God is also present. We must live in accordance to his will and majesty and keep his commandments. It is imperative that we furnish the life so that God can use us. As it is written, I can do all things through Christ who strengthens me.

Love

I came from an era influenced in large part by what can be viewed as the media portrayal of love. *Ozzie and Harriet, Father Knows Best*, etc. Even my parents—the only thing that separated them was death. So, in my naïve way of thinking, I thought when you said *I do*, that was it, all your ducks would automatically be lined up in a row.

So, in terms of love, although it is illusive and difficult at times, it is something that we aspire to have or be a part of. I am impressed with Barack and Michelle Obama. When I see them, I often think that they have raised the bar for Black love. Like most couples, I am sure they have their challenges, but they set out on a mission, and they achieved (and continue to achieve) their objective, which shows the power of being on one accord and staying the course. It's when couples are off track and get lost in the shuffle that they most times don't stay the course. The vows that you take in the marriage ceremony, although a few words, have profound implications. You make a vow to the Lord, and you should not take it back.

What is love? Is it something we say or is it something we do? Do we define it based on what is outside of us as in the case of the media portrayal of it? Or is it based on what we have internalized it to be? Either way it goes, it is something we look forward to experiencing in our life.

When many of us are involved in loving relationships, we expect certain things to be present in them. We know the Hollywood Paradigm that conveys a perpetual romantic mode of existence where everything is everything with few problems or difficulties. But contrary to the popular notion, love tends to either bring out the worst in individuals and or the best. One must be willing to talk about the issues and challenges that you go through in a marriage, for we live in a world that is so contrary to the way that God intended for it to be, and it shows up in our relationships with one another, even our marriages.

It would seem at times that love, and happiness, is an oxymoron, two opposing elements conjoined together. The more you expect from someone, the less you tend to get. In a loving relationship, you expect certain provisions to be made. At best what you get is two opposing wills fighting to advance their own agenda independent of the will of each other.

There are times when there is a mutual accommodation of one another's aspirations, but those reflect exceptional alliances that have risen to the occasion. When you work together for the mutual benefit of one another, you can rise above the impediments of life. I think of Barack and Michelle Obama and what it took for them to get to the White House within the onslaught of criticism and contentious behavior directed toward them. That is my model for excellence. As I stated from the outset of this chapter, is love something we say or something we do. And the bottom line is we need to define love more so along the lines of being an action word. Essentially, it is something we do. It is how we treat one another that does make a difference.

At the end of the day, it is how we have treated one another. Have we done the best to advance the needs of the relationship, or have we pursued our own agenda not considering the needs of one another? It is true that we can say that we love someone, but it is how we treat one another that really makes a difference.

The interesting thing about being in love is that two people have chosen to be together to promote the well-being of one another. Or what that translates into depends upon the needs of the two individuals and what they aspire to achieve.

To overcome your impediments within this contemporary conundrum, one must be willing to go to the next dimension of their thinking. To transcend your thinking, one must give of themselves in a selfless mode. The ultimate measure of love is to love others as you love yourself.

We are put on this earth to be a helpmate to one another and not a hindrance, to bring out the best in one another as opposed to the worst. We are challenged and impeded by so many external factors; nowhere is that more evident in how we treat one another up close and personal.

Loving with a Renewed Mind

There is always room for improvement and a willingness to work on yourself; as it is often quoted, to thy own self be true. There are ongoing challenges that we all contend with, and when you deal with someone up close and personal, one should be willing to do the work. So many people throw in the towel when their marital problems appear unbeatable or overwhelming. My wife and I have our share of challenges as well, which is why I've decided to share my perspective while also doing the work.

That is just the nature of marital relationships. It has not always been easy, and we had to accept that. There are times when your contention is that I didn't sign up for this, and your partner sentiments are the same, but somehow you make it.

To rise above your stumbling blocks in this life, one must focus on elevation and seeking counsel to learn how to grow out of leaning to your own understanding. Harboring feelings of vengeance or being consumed with anger undermines your spiritual integrity and puts you at odds with what God has designed you to do. The truth is we must wholeheartedly trust in the process and let God have his way with us.

We know that there is awesome power in being in love, especially when that love is being directed toward another human being. Oftentimes, we allow someone to be the object of our love, entrusting them with our heart and strongly desiring them to deliver on the promise to value and respect the sanctity of love. We place our trust in that person's hand hoping that they will not cause undue distress to us.

Our expectations of love are so high, for we know in the eyesight of the creator that he expects us to love one another just as he loves us. For God is love, and to experience God is to allow ourselves to be open and willing to the love experience and all that it entails. For the creator loves us regardless of the issues that we allow to adversely affect us. For he knows the greatness that resides in us; he made us in the best of molds. He made us in his image and likeness.

Being that we are made in the form of God, we have the potential to achieve so much, yet we impose so many limitations upon ourselves. As evidenced by our unwillingness to forgive those that we have entrusted our hearts to fall short. At this point, we put ourselves in the dubious position of weakening the integrity of our relationship.

People make a conscious effort to reconcile their relationships, or they choose to surrender without ever working to resolve their problems that bring out the dark side of their relationships. I say all this because on the eve of my 20th anniversary, I was faced with a dilemma of sorts. My wife and I had an ongoing snag in our relationship. Like a lot of couples, we too have our toils and snares to deal with that flare up from time to time.

Even though you come together as one, you are still two unique individuals with completely different ways of handling issues. We must be mindful of who we are and aware of who our partners are. Having this knowledge helps us to understand that we can't raise anyone nor make them into our image or likeness. The prayer is that through how we love we can influence and encourage them to do the work and change as we do the work and change.

When you truly know people and love them regardless of their flaws, it isn't always easy. We must love one another unconditionally and without reservations just as God loves us in spite of our limitations and faults. The problem that we have as humans is that we allow for issues and concerns that are contrary to the loving process to get in the way. Oftentimes, we sabotage the virtue of our relationships by doing things that are counterproductive to the loving processes that we involve ourselves in.

Intrinsically, we put ourselves in a conflictual relationship when we operate in a manner that is contrary to the nature of love. Sometimes, it is not our fault as much as it is the expectations that we have for one another. We choose people with the hope that they will deliver on our expectations and preconceived notions that we have about love right or wrong, leaving us to decide just how and to what depth we love them.

When a Man Finds a Wife, He Finds a Good Thing

Marriage has proven to be, by far, the most interesting and challenging relationship that I have had with any one person. Throughout the course of time, my feelings have run the gamut from ecstatic to how did I get into this relationship and what was I thinking. In the spiritual realm, it has afforded me an opportunity to develop a closer relationship with the creator because it caused me to go to the next dimension in my thinking.

Marriage is a very selfless act. I was accustomed to being in a caring and sharing posture. The distinction for me now is the unconditional love that you are more cognizant of in the eyesight of God. Marriage afforded me the opportunity to extend love to someone in the similitude as God loving us unconditionally because he extends his mercy and grace upon us.

As a contemporary writer put these words in a song: "the true measure of love is love without measure." In the same context, I must make mention of the notion presented by a great poet: "I am a movement by myself, but I am a force when we are together."

I have really come to appreciate my wife and the fact that she complements me in its entirety. These past few years have not been easy for me or my family. In a time when there is a need for surety, we have been faced with a lot of uncertainty. I have been marginally employed, and there have been times when she has been off work due to illness or limitations, which have adversely impacted her ability to work.

Also, this has not taken into account a myriad of incidental events that impacted our family. But through it all, we have clung to one another.

I know my wife is truly a blessing to me, and she has significantly figured into my spiritual elevation and has enriched my life many times over. It is often stated that behind every great man there is a great woman. I spend the greater part of my day uplifting and motivating others, and at the end of the day, when all is said and done, in addition to leaning on the Lord, I must acknowledge and give a lot of credit to my wife as the proverbial helpmate. Oftentimes, it seems like she is more effective in implementing my ideas than what I am.

The most important part of an idea is making it tangible, and some of us are more effective in the transmutation process. By my own admission, I am a dreamer, which has a significant place in the scheme of things. But there comes a time when that idea manifests and become a reality. It is important that your creativity manifest itself and becomes your reality to be successful in life. Essentially, you need to go beyond the drawing board or should we say the dream state. It is a known fact that many of us have great ideas, but the person who brings that idea to the market will get the recognition for it.

Where I may initiate a lot of ideas, it is my wife who makes it an accomplished fact. Verbiage is only as good as the associated actions that allow for it to manifest. My wife has proven to be my trusted confidante and friend. I can rely on her many times over in the midst of overwhelming adversity.

She has been a pillar to lean on. One of the contemporary artists put those words in a loving song when he stated in endearing terms to the object of his affection: "I would rather go through hard times with you than good times with someone else." Not every couple can handle the extreme diverse complications that befall individuals from time to time. In any relationship, it's not just what you go through, but how the two of you come together to weather the storms that makes the difference. What has always given me hope is that God has the final say in all affairs, and our best bet is to work on being the best that we can be.

Dr. Martin Luther King Jr. stated, "The true test of man's character is not how he does when times are going good, but it is how he prevails during adversity." Oftentimes, people say that when they had plenty of money, everyone was their friend, but when their money ran out, so did their friends. As Bobby Womack sang in his song: "Nobody wants you when you're down and out." It's the ones who stick by you when you are consumed with fear and your life is full of uncertainty who are important. When you can't fight and you're in an emotional quagmire, it's the people who come to your aid that truly make a difference.

My wife stated something to me one day that was so poignant and clear: you have spent so much time advising others. Now is the time to take your own advice. This came at a time in life when I really couldn't see the forest for the trees. I was drowning in sorrow and grieving over the way my life was going. I had made a career change, and things were not going well for me.

Essentially, she gave me a dose of reality that was plain and clear:

stop looking for others to validate you and have more faith in yourself. Even my daughter said basically the same thing. For things to get better for me, I needed someone like me to help me get to the next level.

My wife encourages me to go farther than I do to continue to challenge myself and most importantly to not only follow my dreams but to make my dreams my reality. Others have encouraged me as well, but my wife tends to recognize that not only do I need a nudge but maybe I need a kick in the butt at times. I truly am grateful for her patience and understanding. One thing I know is that it has not been easy for her being married to the man of her dreams who also tends to be a dreamer, but I have learned more about God by her doing so. My wife recognizes the value of the biblical verse "without a vision the people perish." My wife recognized the skills and talents that I have early in our relationship. Her role is to aid me in actualizing or manifesting my dreams, to aid me in becoming the man that I am destined to become.

Someone believing in you is wonderful, but the most important thing is for you to believe in yourself to the same extent. Many years ago, someone acknowledged the skills and talents that I have, and I just dismissed what he stated as a casual remark. But his comments have taken on so much more significance with the passage of time. He stated that you can't see yourself the way others see you. Even now, people watch and comment on my actions, and while their comments are admirable, there is something missing in the equation.

I often sense that there is a certain level of doubt or insecurity that I must overcome that is keeping me from reaching the level of excellence to achieve my objective. So poised and confident when it comes to edifying others, but I consistently impose limits on myself.

I come across in such radiant and glowing terms, but I fizzle out just as quickly.

My wife encourages me, she tells me that this is my season, that now is the time to grab life by the brass ring and manifest my aspirations. If God has promised me, why should I hinder the process? She admires my intellectual, philosophical anecdotes that I spew out from time to time. But at the same time, all of that is in vain if there aren't any corresponding actions. Biblically speaking, "faith without works is dead." Learn the value of leaning on the Lord and not your own understanding.

It is imperative that one live a spirit-filled life and recognize that God is our inexhaustible vein of supply. Oftentimes, I am reminded of the biblical decree where we are encouraged to meditate on God's word day and night. What readily comes to mind is the biblical concept: "for those that the Lord calls he qualifies them." We all have gifts and talents that the Lord has given us, and as the Bible states, your gifts and talents will make a way for you. My wife reminds me of that; if God has decreed a matter, then consider it a done deal. Doubting yourself is one thing, but you should never doubt God.

The beauty of marriage comes when she stays by your side and loves you despite your foolishness and folly, bears your children, and stays with you despite issues and trials and tribulations. She contends with you even when others have counted you out.

Because she recognizes your intrinsic good and encourages you and reminds you how awesome you are, because she sees you through the eyes of God, she prays for you, so see yourself as God sees you as well. She knows what God knows because God has embedded this conscious within her.

God sanctions marriage as a relationship to exceed all relationships. We are instructed to meditate on the word day and night. "Because of sexual immorality, God decreed that every man should have his own wife and that every wife should have their own husband." We should not be led astray by our own devices. Marriage is the wing nut that holds our civilization together. It is imperative that we channel ourselves in the proper manner and focus on long term, enduring relationships, and bring out the best in one another.

Don't Give Up

In any endeavor, it's important that you think outside of the box and examine yourself paying attention to self-inflicted limitations. It wasn't until I started stepping outside of my personal box that I began confronting my own fears and issues with doubt. I am a mental health technician, and I spend the greater part of my day inspiring and motivating others to improve their own mental healthcare. It would be paradoxical of me if I didn't pursue my aspirations as well as work to improve my own mental health. If the teacher doesn't pursue their dreams, then how effective can one be as a teacher?

We operate outside of the will of God when we allow our fears and doubts to consume us. In my case, I had to take a leap of faith and confront my insecurities, perceived or otherwise. To plant something in you, you have to allow the process to work. For God will give you the desires of your heart as he works through you.

One must be mindful of the fact, as Henry Ford stated, that whether you think you can or you think you can't you are right. The way we think has profound influences on how we behave. You can tell the winners coming out the gate. When you know better, you do better. As we evolve in our consciousness and our awareness of things in the spirit, we gain a greater appreciation of ourselves despite ourselves.

In Romans 5, we find the following verse: "but we also glory in tribulations, knowing that tribulation produces perseverance; and perseverance, character, and character hope." It is hard to concede to defeat knowing that you have not exhausted all your options. If we don't move past the tribulations, we never produce perseverance, character, and hope. Case in point, I get frustrated with my circumstances, and to no avail the more I try, the more difficult it gets. I had to overcome my fears and doubts and not undermine myself.

Renowned motivational speaker Les Brown stated it took him 13 years to overcome his fears and doubts to step out on faith. Through this renewing experience, I am finding out that it is a process. I am now more conscious of what it means to be a hearer of the word as well as a doer. But it is stated we must have the faith of a mustard seed, a small seed that produces the mighty yield.

We must remember who we are and whose we are. We are made in the image and likeness of God. We were made in the best of molds, with a specific plan and purpose for our lives. Sometimes hearing who and what we are on a constant basis is the only thing that stands between us believing and manifesting or not.

At times, it would appear that we are of a lesser construct from the vantage point of being human. We come to believe we have limited potential. But we have unlimited potential in the divine mind of Christ. Christ is the knowledge and wisdom of God unto salvation. We are told to let this mind be in you that was also in Christ Jesus who being a form of God did consider it robbery to be equal with God.

We must lean on the Lord and not our own understanding and trust in him with all our might so that he will direct our path.

The most powerful word in the human lexicon is "let"; once we let the process work, we will do better. Christ is the mind of God individualized. We are God's manifestation and expression here on earth.

We are the personification of God. God needed something to house his spirit in, so he made man. We are spiritual beings experiencing the human condition. We are not human beings with spiritual inclinations. Our greater component is our spirituality.

Never forget that greater is he that is in you than he that is in the world. Our level of thinking is what either makes us or breaks us. As a man thinks in his heart so is he. Our thoughts are a self-fulfilling prophecy. Thoughts are things and words materialize. The creator holds us responsible for our words, thoughts, and deeds.

We must be in alignment with the will of the creator always and operate as if we are in the very presence of God. We can't see God, but we know for a surety that he sees us. We are to live a life consistent with a Godly nature irrespective to any circumstances.

Living a life contrary to the will of God causes one to be separated from God and outside of the will of God, resulting in a reprobate mind. We can justify anything that we do that works for us when we agree with God. Conversely, when we are outside the will of God, we foster an adversarial relationship with God, subjecting ourselves to a life of chaos and destruction.

The road to perdition is paved with good intentions. We must rise above the human eclipsiation of life and lean more on the divine mind of Christ.

Christ is the consciousness that Jesus personified and so can we. As it is written, Jesus stated great things have I done but greater things shall you do. During adversity, we must remind ourselves that this is not as good as it gets. No, the best is yet to come. I can do all things through Christ who strengthens me.

Don't give up. As it is stated, no retreat, no surrender. Failure is not an option, for we are more than a conqueror. For God decreed that we are Dominionites, which means we have supreme authority over everything. Before we can have authority over anything, we must exert authority over ourselves.

Once again, we are responsible for the thoughts that we entertain. Mind your mind, think about what you think about. In the wisdom of the elders, it is stated we are not to entertain thoughts that are contrary to the will of God. The process is likened to a letter that comes to your home that is not yours. You are instructed to not open it and to return to the sender. Such is the case with impure thoughts; don't hold on to them. Send them back out into the universe.

The thoughts that we entertain have such a profound impact on our well-being. The battle is in our mind; everything is preceded by the consciousness that precipitated it. Thoughts are things and words materialize. We must be cognizant of how we think. Our condition does not change until our level of thinking does. The ancient Sanskrit word for man means to think, but it is how and what thoughts that we entertain that matter. Whether you think you can or you can't, you're right. Once again, your perception of yourself is so important.

We are not to be conformed to the world but transformed by the renewal of the mind. Let this mind be in you that was also in Christ Jesus. As a man thinks in his heart so is he. Thoughts are things and words materialized. Lean on the Lord and not your own understanding. Man's knowledge pales in comparison to God's. We can do all things through Christ who strengthens us. Christ is the mind of God individualized. God breathed into the nostril of man and made him a living soul. We are not mere human beings with spiritual inclinations; to the contrary, we are spiritual beings experiencing the human condition. This is not as good as it gets. The best is yet to come. We are God's manifestation and expression here on earth.

So much has been said about how we think in a manner independent of the will of God, but now it is time to demonstrate a consciousness to be in alignment with the will of God. We can do all things through Christ who strengthens us. As Jesus stated, the Father and I are one. We are a manifestation and expression of God. We're made in his image, and we do ourselves a grave disservice and suffer needlessly when we live a life contrary to the will of God. We must resolve to keep the faith and hold on to God's unchanging hands, knowing that he can resolve any issue that we have. Doubting ourselves is one thing, but doubting the God that is in us is another.

Don't give up; failure is not an option for a believer, for we are more than a conqueror. We have an opportunity to live a Christ-centered life that provides strength and hope for our days to come. When we give up, we are operating outside of the will of God in contrast to our very nature. God decreed that we have dominion over everything, that everything is subservient to man.

We have supreme authority over any entity. But first and foremost, we must be in alignment with the will of God.

Irrespective to appearance of things and what seems to be improbable, God has the final say in all matters for man plans and God plans, but God is the best of planners. Some things seem insurmountable in the human realm, but in the divine mind of

Christ, we have unlimited potential. As it is written, I can do all things through Christ that strengthens me. Christ is the knowledge and wisdom of God unto salvation. Christ is the mind of God individualized.

We must become new creatures in Christ. Once we recognize and realize our divinity and start living a Christ-centered existence, we tap into a Christ like or Godlike attributes. As Jesus stated, the Father and I are one. Our oneness with God is our salvation to agree irrespective to what the circumstances to acknowledge him in all your endeavors.

Lean on the Lord and not your own understanding, and trust in him with all your might, and he will direct your path. Be as Job and display unwavering faith amid mountainous situations; we must be mindful that there is no failure with God. We serve an awesome God, and we are made in his image and likeness. As such, we are a form of God. God made man in his image and likeness—formed him from the dust of the ground and breathed into his nostrils and made him a living soul. God made man in the best of molds, made him a little lower than the angels.

It is time to rise above the human obstructions, and lean more on the divine mind of Christ; we all are endowed with the Christ potential. The challenge that we are faced with is whether we will let the process work or do the Will of God.

Don't let anything separate you from the love of God. We're not to be conformed to the world but be transformed by the renewal of our mind. Like Job, in spite of seemingly insurmountable or mountainous situations, we must display Spiritual Integrity, to know beyond a shadow of doubt that God has a way out for the faithful.

Change

When you want change, it seems like things can't change fast enough. But what one must be cognizant of is that nothing changes until your perspective changes. Your circumstances will not change until the way you think about them changes.

Dr. Keefa, through a question, pointed out something that eluded me: what was I holding back when people hear me speak? Through this encounter, I realized that not only was it my own fear, but also that I owed God an apology for neglecting my ministry. Oftentimes, we are not able to see things within ourselves until those that care about us bring it to our attention.

I recognized that rising above the self-doubt was something that freed me and helped me become the man who had dominion over fear. There is no way I can change my position until I elevate my thinking. When I think about my stature, I should be much further ahead. As the Bible states, I am suffering needlessly.

I think about countless others who have preceded me who have accomplished so much; they had to start somewhere. I began to see that I had to put myself in the proximity of what I desire to achieve. It is time to stop playing the armchair quarterback and get in the game. EVERYONE STARTS AT THE BEGINNING; EVERYONE HAS TO CONFRONT THEIR OBSTACLES.

For me, I must nurture this desire and let it manifest and do what my beloved minister tells us to do: "to rise above the human eclipsiation of life and lean more on the divine mind of Christ," for Christ is the knowledge and wisdom of God unto salvation.

As renowned theologian Eric Butterworth states in *Discover the Power within You*: "Although we are limited in the human realm we have unlimited potential in the divine mind of Christ."

With the knowledge and insight that I have acquired, it really is no excuse that I can legitimize my fear, for fear is false evidence appearing real. As much time and attention that I devote to restructuring and elevating others, I should consider myself as worthy of the same edification.

"Delight yourself also in the Lord and he shall give you the desires of your heart." I need to be mindful that God put my vision on my heart, and as Les Brown stated, God gave me this assignment for a reason, and it is intended to come through me. So, doubting myself really is doubting the God in me. I must trust in the process and let God have his way with me. As a servant of the Lord, I must be a willing instrument of his will, and let his spirit resonate through me.

The scenarios are likened to the Prophet Jonah who disobeyed the commandment of God and was cast overboard and ended up in the belly of the whale. His doubt and disobedience brought him unnecessary misfortune. Again, this makes me think of Dr. Keefa, who stated I owed God an apology by not giving my ministry the attention that it deserved. Not only do I suffer the misfortune of my fear, but the people I help do, too. Actually, it sounds like I need to offer God *two* apologies.

Least I forget that just like God has planted a vision within me, he could very well give the assignment to someone else worthier of the task. That is the thing that I should fear, to lose the favor of the Lord because I was a reluctant warrior or servant of God. Now, I have devoted so much of my time and energy in my personal development.

I cannot let it be in vain. For those that the Lord calls, he gives them the qualifications.

As it is written, God will give you the desires of your heart, for the very thing that you desire is the very thing that God intends for you. It is a circular matter. God intends for his needs to be met because we are the expression and manifestation of God.

If God decrees a matter, then why should we attempt to usurp God, for it is written that man's knowledge pales in comparison to God? We are instructed to lean on the Lord and not our own understanding and to trust in him with all our might and that he will direct our path.

For God not only rules, but he super rules, for he has the final say in all matters. Be mindful that there is no failure with God. We are to agree with God and to not let anything separate us from God. As Jesus stated, the Father and I are one.

We are to live as if we are in the very presence of God and to live a Christ-centered life. To be Christ like means to be Godlike. Not only should I expound this consciousness, but I should demonstrate it as well. There should be no distinction between what I say and what I do.

We serve an awesome God that does anything but fail. We must acknowledge that we do nothing of ourselves except it be revealed to us by God. Give God the glory and acknowledge him in all your ways. Being ever so mindful that man's knowledge pales in comparison to God's, that man is nothing but a mere vapor in the absence of God. Real change comes when we allow God to direct our path and lean on him and not our own understanding.

We should not live a life separate or contrary to the will of God.

Remember to Remember

It is so important to lean on the Lord and not your own understanding, for if one walks by sight and not by faith, you will miss the big picture. Be mindful of this fact and let it marinate in your soul: man's knowledge pales in comparison to the knowledge of God.

We have come this far by faith and trusting in the creator, for he made a way out of no way. The Lord will put no more on you than what you can bear; he will leave the way of escape for the faithful. For lest we forget, faith is the substance of things hoped for and the evidence of things unseen.

It takes a greater awareness of the power that resides within you. As Jesus stated: "he that believes in that which is in me great things have I done; but greater things shall you do." For it is only after the storm that one really appreciates the sunshine. As it is written, it rains on the just and the unjust. I know within my heart that the Lord truly has been a wonder in my life, and I have come this far by faith. The Lord has truly brought me from a mighty long way out of the darkness into the marvelous light.

Faith triumphs amid adversity. We are a byproduct of our experiences, the good times or the things which were not so pleasant. As it is written, had it not been for the storm, I would not know how to appreciate the sunshine in the manner that it is supposed to be appreciated. At times we take ourselves and one another for granted, and that is easy to do in the scheme of things.

We either minimize ourselves and undervalue our assets or accentuate our deficiencies.

A recurring theme for me is that all things come in time, and things can and will work themselves out; we cannot rush the process. It is incumbent upon us to rely on the divine wisdom that resides within us to guide and direct our path. We must be doers of the word not just hearers of the word. It is our time; we must let our light shine so that others can see our good works.

We must demonstrate our faith and not just verbalize it; as it is written, we are to furnish the life so that God can use us. There is divine sovereignty that exists in the universe, and it also exists within us as well, for we emanate from a mighty source. We are made in the image and likeness of God. As such, we are a form of God. We must remain steadfast in our convictions and hold on to God's unchanging hands and know for a fact that God is no respecter of persons. What he has done for others, you can rest assure that he will do for you. Just like God is patient with us, we must learn (or relearn) how to be patient with ourselves.

How else can we be new creatures in Christ unless we live in accordance to the will of almighty God? We must ask God for deliverance.

Daddy's Little Girls

My daughters are not little, and they are not girls; they are grown women, but I refer to them as that because of the endearing relationship that we have. As I have always said, not only did I raise my daughters, but my daughters raised me. A thought I entertained in my youth that became my benchmark for what I aspired to do is that I was always conscientious of how I treated someone else's daughter because of how I viewed my daughters. Most importantly, I wanted to be respected by others, so I respected women because I felt that was the natural thing to do.

Some would say it is the nature of a man to go astray and be indifferent to women. To the contrary, it's the nature of a man to bring forth the best in a woman and protect her, give her reassurance so that she in turn could extend that to him. **AS IT IS WRITTEN, DO ONTO OTHERS AS YOU WOULD HAVE THEM DO ON TO YOU. ADDITIONALLY, A NATION CANNOT RISE ABOVE THE LEVEL OF HOW THEY TREAT THEIR WOMEN.** As a nation, we are obligated to treat the women in the best manner that brings forth their intrinsic good and provide the environment that is most conducive for that. In that respect, we really have fallen short.

Some of the things that my daughters have told me that I have instilled in them make me chuckle, but they are all true. Just as I am indebted to my daughters, they feel indebted to me as well. I have high expectations of them and have always encouraged them to do their best and don't let anyone misuse or demean them. You're not common, and don't view yourself as such.

There are themes of self-persecution or denigration that are common with today's women: video vixens, on and off the screen, dressing scantily clad and too provocatively and being okay with that; promiscuity and loose morals; hanging from poles and being too liberal with their body and being okay with it. The women of today have given away the milk, so men don't have to buy the cow. Now women wonder why men are not marrying them.

It is not easy for the women, nor is it easy for any of us, but we still can display integrity and hold on to what we believe and to what sustained us when we did not have as much as we do now. **WE STILL HAVE A MORAL OBLIGATION TO DO THE RIGHT THING AND TO DO WHAT IS PLEASING IN THE EYESIGHT OF THE LORD.** For the Lord gave us a gift, our life, and we are to cherish it. Not only is our life a gift, but God allows us to have a life so that we can glorify him and not ourselves. For God expects a lot out of us, and we are obligated to serve him irrespective to circumstances or the appearance of things. As a wise man and mentor told me, the greatest thing you give your children is their spiritual awareness. Like Kahlil Gibran stated, your children come through you, but they belong to God.

The remarkable thing about my daughters is that they raised my level of awareness about how to live and how to treat people. As it is often stated by countless others, including myself, there is no book that really prepares you for parenting; it definitely is trial by fire. Even with the best of intentions, mistakes will happen, but it's your intentions that matter. As a young parent, I did the best that I knew how to do, but I must admit with the help of the Lord and countless others, I made it. I am especially indebted to my daughters' grandmother Helen, for her presence made all the difference in the world. For in the absence of my mother, she was both a mother to me and my daughters.

My daughters often tell me how grateful they were for me being a part of their life, but I remind them that I was so grateful that they were part of my life as well; it was a winning situation for all of us. God always knows what is best for us, for man plans and God plans, but God is the best of planners. Although I lost my mother at a young age, my daughters provided that unconditional love that I needed, for there was a time when I felt so low and uncertain of myself or my future, but the presence of my daughters made all the difference in the world.

Having emotional and psychological challenges at the tender age of 21 then experiencing another episode at 24 at a time when I didn't have a clear definition of who I was or what I was, I was devastated, to say the least. I was a shattered individual who felt so overwhelmed by my circumstances I did not have a clue of how to change, but I knew I had to get it together. I had a family of my own to take care of. Even though I was a noncustodial parent, my children were a source of delight and inspiration. They valued me, and I valued them as well.

The remarkable thing about being a father is that it is a great opportunity to love and be loved. In return, the look that young children give to their parents, it's like they say parents are the center of their children's universe. Just their presence gives reassurance that all is well in their world. Fathers that abandon their children don't realize that they miss a treat not being a part of their children's life. My daughters said how much they enjoyed and benefited from being a part of my life. Well, I can tell you emphatically the feelings are mutual. Being a young father forced me to make decisions that allowed me to become the person I am today.

The summer before I started my first semester of college, I met someone, fell head over heels in love, and next thing I knew, we had a baby on the way. Now that was not the way my father and I had mapped things out. I was on track to become a lawyer; that was our plan. Having a baby right out the gate was not the way it was planned, but Denise and I had worked it out in our thinking. We knew we would be together, so having a baby was an added feature.

Interesting as I write about this odyssey of self-discovery, this is the time of year that it unfolded: the summer of 1973. The ensuing fall I was going away to Michigan State University en route to become a lawyer with a baby on the way. What a recipe for transformation, a point in time that would change my life and impact me for years to come. It's stated that if you want to make God laugh show him your plans. I was the example for this statement.

YOUNG LOVE IS NOT TO BE TAKEN FOR GRANTED OR DISMISSED AS SOMETHING FOOLISH. I KNOW WHAT I FELT, AND YES, IT WAS WORTH IT IN SPITE OF THE EVENTS THAT UNFOLDED. Denise and I believed in one another and the power of love, for if we didn't we never would have pursued the course that we did. I can't fault her or myself for things not working out. We just met at a time when we didn't know how powerful love can be and that it can be self-sustaining despite anything to the contrary. I have learned to respect the power of love.

When I reflect on the decisions I've made in my life, I think about how I was conflicted about going away to Michigan State in the weeks preceding leaving, but there was a part of me that was determined to have this baby. Had I chosen to go to Wayne State University instead, I would have missed the lessons and blessings that God had designed for my life. I knew that being too close to home would have been too overwhelming. I didn't know how I was going to tell my parents, but my younger brother Wesley blurted it out to my mother at the kitchen table before I could muster up the courage to say anything. And FYI, I will be eternally grateful to Wesley for that gesture. Lord knows I didn't know what to say or do.

I have met so many people who started out young like I was that prevailed over things and made it. One admirable couple whom I take delight and worth emulating is my niece and her significant other. Bobby and Eula have been together for an extended period and convey what Black love is all about. Bobby and Eula are the prototype of what can be if you only believe. I appreciate having such models in young people that I can admire and learn from to apply in my own life.

I always encourage clients that if they can't talk about how they feel they should write about it because writing is cathartic. This is an experience that is worth bringing forth because of the direction that my life went because of these events and the consciousness that evolved from it. For that, not only am I well pleased, but God is pleased as well. My brother Abdul tells me that I came out a better person because of the experience.

So, with a baby on the way and an idea planted in my head by my eldest brother William, off to college I went. During our many late-night discussions, which went on into the wee hours of the morning, we expressed and explored things, and he encouraged me to become a lawyer. I immediately told my father. He was elated and assured me that we could do it.

This is a very sensitive matter, but is the type of stuff that must be expressed. Most times people are faced with so many challenges that they don't know what to do, but it's them believing that helps them prevail over mountainous situations. When asked about what led to my first breakdown, my father stated that it was the events that transpired during my time at Michigan State University.

I was determined to make it despite being estranged from my parents and not knowing how to verbalize my needs to others. I had pretty much isolated myself from the other students at school and put all my energies into my studies. This was not so complicated the first year of school, but it did not work out the second year of school.

The most important thing that we have is our faith and our belief that we will prevail at the end of the journey. For me, I always believed in doing the right thing. I didn't know any other way of doing things. My parents had such a stronghold on me at times I felt that they were smothering me, but I believed in them. I was the one whom they expected so much from, and I was determined to meet their expectations and everyone else's as well as mine.

No one understands the way that God does, for truly he was watching over me at this juncture in time. I did not know the Lord, but he knew me and brought me through the tumultuous relationship that I had with myself. If it wasn't God on my side, where would I be?

When I met Denise, she had a little girl name Katrina, and I was so impressed with her from the start. It is so interesting when I look back on that period. It is often stated that you know where you have been, but you never know how things are going to unfold.

Katrina was a baby when I met her; she was not even walking or talking when I met her, so at a later point in time when Denise and I broke up, so many people would ask or say that I was only obligated to one child, but I beg to differ; a deal was brokered between the Lord, mother Helen (Katrina's grandmother), and myself that although I was not her father I was the father Katrina would come to know. Just as in the absence of my mother and because of her needs, I was the son Helen needed as well.

There were intense challenges that Mother Helen had to deal with on many levels, but when she introduced me to her friends and acquaintances, she took special delight in telling them that I was going to college. There was a kinship that Mother Helen and I shared that stood the test of time, and the only thing that separated us was death. The interesting thing is as awkward as I was, she could relate to me, and I could relate to her. During the early phases of our relationship, we trusted one another and just watched things unfold.

As it is often stated, you know where you been, but you have no idea what is around the bend, especially when you are young and naïve to the ways of the world as well as not having a clear definition of who you are or in the spiritual realm what you are in the eyesight of God. God doesn't put any more on you than what you can bear, and he will leave a way of escape for the faithful. The most consistent relationship that I have had has been my relationship with my daughters. For 40 years, we have watched over one another and dealt with one another from afar and up close.

I am eternally grateful for my daughters simply because everything that happened to me and for me was born out of the decision to become a father at the time that I did. God has a way of letting you know that he has his loving arms of protection around you and adds surety to your existence; one must be discerning to see and feel his presence. Although abortion was remotely considered, it was ruled out early in the game. At Michigan State during my travels across campus, I ran across the College of Natural Science. I like to think God put this school in my path to show his might.

For in that school, there was a display that showed the various phases of a baby's development from an embryo through the whole sequential order up to nine months. As the pregnancy progressed, I was able to see how the baby looked inside the belly of Denise. I just marveled at the process and what was unfolding inside of her. As things went on, I did not know how to discuss the matter with my parents. I didn't share the experience with anyone at all. Not even a dear friend of mine, Dean Johnson. In my way of thinking, I did not want to be deterred or discouraged from having this baby. I was naïve and ignorant of certain processes, but I was determined to make it.

I encourage people all the time to address their issues and concerns and do it in a manner that brings forth the best for all parties. I also encourage people to confront themselves as it is stated in the AA meetings, take fearless inventory of yourself. From my experience, I learned the value of this process because I did not know how to deal with things from this vantage point, nor did I know that this was a viable option for me.

There would come a time when I would not only be at odds with others but also with myself as well, for when you don't know, things come with a price. It's in the midst of while you're going through things that God will reveal himself to you and make himself evident if one has a sense of discernment about himself. On reflection, God was ever present in my life; I was just too grievous to see his presence.

It was not just that others didn't understand my needs. I had lost perspective on what my needs were.

Once again, having a child at that time in my life was a conscious decision that I made; there was intense love for her mother and the need to deal with the matter in an honorable way. I could have dealt with the subsequent matter differently. But that was the nature of my understanding at the time. I had my set of challenges and was determined to prevail. I did not understand the spiritual implications of what I was going through, nor did I know about the power of prayer. On reflection, I did know that there were some prayer warriors involved in my quest.

As difficult as the matter proved to be, I felt vindicated that the child was born on my mother's birthday. That was a reminder that God was watching over me and had his loving arms of protection around me. It's when you go through something and you look back over things that you end up singing a hymn of praise like "how you never would have made without the Lord on your side." You come to realize just how powerful God really is. It is at those times when I recognized God at work in my life and my ability to use what I learned from my experiences became easier.

I know that God allowed me to go through what I did, for it proved to be my testimony. There is no testimony without a test, and today I have God to thank for my daughters being the representations of my testimony and the victories I won while passing through those difficult times.

Letters to the Constellation

Dear Elijah

I write this inquiry because when I look at you I see something, and I feel a presence in you that is a cause of concern. You always have had a distinct flavor about you that was both appealing and troubling. I have watched you over the years, and as I look back at your growth and development, I saw certain things, but the parent in me was trusting that everything would be all right. But as I look back at you, considering how you are now, I should have paid more attention to you.

By my own admission, you were so precious to me I did not want to see any flaw in you remotely or otherwise. Being that you were my first-born son, to have you after all these years in my life I am thankful. There was a time in my life when I sustained so many losses in the bringing forth of a child. After dealing with the grief of countless miscarriages, you were the byproduct of something that preceded your presence in ways far richer than words could explain. Not only were you conceived, but in a way, you were a gift from God.

You were a corrective entry in my life from someone of my past who was unable to deliver a child. You were also a corrective entry in my life because my father needed you to be here because he knew he wouldn't be with us as much as he would have liked to have been, for his journey was soon to end. In many ways, the universe smiled upon your arrival to your journey. You have a mission to fulfill to the universe; that is why there are so many hostile forces trying to sabotage your mission.

The male child is so important to the human family. When we look around at the devastation that has taken hold of our community and at large, it is because of the dismal state of the Black man. So many young Black men have fallen through the safety net. We know that a lot of it is by design and the genocidal snares that have been put in our path consistently down through the years. But we also know that these issues come from their own doings: rejecting education, adopting countercultural and defiant actions like the youths of preceding generations. But for some reason, it has taken an unprecedented stronghold on our community like never.

So many of our youth like you have allowed themselves to be easily misled by their own devices. They allow themselves to be defined as a product of their environment with the major focus on the undesirable qualities of their environment being their defining traits. Many of them embrace a culture that is more defined by others than their allegiance to their ancestral lineage and the aspirations of a spiritual connection that seems to have lost its hold on a people that relied upon it so much when it seemed like that was their only hope to sustain them.

Now like so many youth and the youth of preceding generations, there is a sense of reckless defiance that permeates our society, and now the rallying point of one generation has become the battle cry of this generation but with a different twist. One generation expounded liberation by any means necessary. Now, this generation cries out for commercial gain by any means necessary.

So, when we see the restlessness and disillusionment of youth, we must in certain respects embrace them because they exhibit the same conviction to their cause that we did and those who preceded us as well.

It is most important that, like our predecessors, we be there to help guide and direct their actions, and as our parents did, we must love them unconditionally. We pray that as they travel the path of least resistance that in their turbulence they should eventually respond to reason. That their defiance should somehow be a force that can be used to generate more dialogue among us as a people.

Lest we forget, one generation lays the framework for the generation to follow. The generation that gave birth to this generation was just as turbulent as the present one. The children of the '60s that came of age brought with them their own youthful indiscretions, which were a thorn in the side for their parents: the wide spread use of illicit drugs, the lax attitude about sexual relations, the increasing music influence on the youth as their mode of expressing their frustrations, and the challenge to conventional wisdoms and authority figures.

When the Bible states that there is nothing new up under the sun, that is so evident by the fact that one generation comes and other passes away, but the earth endures forever. Again, the outer appearances have changed, but the human condition has remained the same. There has always been a sense of restlessness that has permeated our society and an urgent need for correction or should we say a corrective entry.

I address this letter to my son, but my son is the prototype of countless other children in the father-son construct liken to the prodigal son and his father. Like so many fathers who want their sons to stay on the straight and narrow path. Or in contemporary terms to not jump off the porch too soon. I always told my children that they have a lifetime to be an adult, to enjoy their years as children.

Dear Antoine
January 27, 2006

I know it is difficult for you at this time, but we must be ever so mindful that God is still in control of all matters. At times like this when we're faced with overwhelming odds, it seems like God has forsaken us, and we are prone to question our situation. We still must stand our ground and remain steadfast in our convictions. As we our taught in the Dominion, God is our inexhaustible vein of supply. God truly didn't bring us this far to leave us alone.

We still must learn the value of leaning on the Lord and not our own understanding. Many people have gone through seemingly insurmountable situations in which the very foundations of their faith were tested. But we must be ever so mindful of how the Bible describes faith: "faith is the substance of things hoped for and the evidence of things unseen." Fortunately for you, unlike so many people, you already know the Lord. When you know the Lord, you can testify to his goodness despite appearances. As our elders so aptly put it: "God has a way of making a way out of no way."

Even more to the point: "When a door is closed, a window is

open." One more, young brother: "When you have faith in the Lord, he will open a door that no man can close."

We must be ever so mindful of the awesome power of God and the ever-increasing understanding of what being a child of God allows you to be privy to. The Bible speaks to us as being joint heirs with Jesus. Jesus was anointed with the Christ consciousness because he recognized that he and the Father were one. He recognized the fact as the Bible stated in Genesis: "When God breathed in to the nostrils of Adam he made him a living soul." Be ever so mindful that the spirit of the Lord resides within you.

The goodness of God should forever radiate through us. As stated in song and as Jesus refers to: "this little light of mine, I am going to let it shine, my God gave it to me, everywhere I go I am going to let it shine." When we recognize and realize the intrinsic power of God that resides within us and that God is omnipresent, we allow ourselves to be privy to the bountiful blessings that God has in store for us. For God intends for us to have a full and abundant life.

One of the songs that stands out from my early days in the Universal Triumph the, Dominion, sung so passionately by Rev. Princess Marie Boatman, was "I'll Let Nothing Separate Me from the Love of God." Don't be separated from God. Separate yourself from those things that our contrary to the will of God. We should not go against the will of God. There is a reason why the Bible so clearly states, "We should shun the very presence of evil." If you remember the story of the prodigal son, the main point of the story is that God allows us to exercise our "free will," but it is his express desire that we should do things in accordance with his will. When we deviate from the course, we pay a tremendous price.

The prodigal son realized the error of his ways and returned to his father's house. We should always be open to correction and be ever so mindful of the fact that the Lord has a way of getting our attention. As the Bible states, "For whom the Lord loves he chastises."

Anyone can be redeemed. God encourages us to come back into the fold. The love of our heavenly father is so strong, and he is so forgiving that he gives us ample time to come back into the fold. Even in our errant ways, we should not allow our short sightedness to distance ourselves from God. The prodigal realized the foolishness and folly of his ways. Subsequently, he returned to his father's house and asked for forgiveness. We all must go to God for something, as Lord Shaffer often reminds me. Again, a song that comes to my mind: "if it wasn't for God on my side, where would I be"; God forgives us, but we must learn to forgive ourselves.

Sometimes, we become so consumed with shame and doubt that we exclude the construct of forgiveness from the equation. We allow ourselves to be defined by someone or something external when we should be defining ourselves based on what God has decreed for us. We are made in the image and likeness of God.

Be still and let the Lord work a wonder in your life. It is said in psychology that we use only 10 percent of our brain and within us is untapped mental processes. Correspondingly, when we are unaware of the awesome power that resides within us, we deprive ourselves of hidden resources that could make our lives so much richer. We should express our gratitude to God often. That is why it is imperative that we seek out refuge in him always.

A contemplative life where we explore the inner recesses of our mind is a critical need that we should address always. Allow yourself to be a new creature in Christ, go beyond the self-imposed limitations and accept the unlimited potential that you have inside of you.

Lord Shaffer often reminds us to "Lift up your mind and Christ will set you free." It is often asked what Christ is, and it has been defined to us as "as the knowledge and wisdom of God until salvation." The beauty of the Christ consciousness is that God allows everyone to have privy to it. It is an all-inclusive process. Everyone who submits to the will of God and keeps his commandments is a benefactor of God's goodness. The two commandments that God wants us to embrace above all things are: to love the Lord with thy entire mind, heart, soul, and strength; and to love thy neighbor as you love yourself. Love is the key and a respect for the sanctity of life and all of God's creations. We must recognize and realize that despite our errant ways that God still loves.

God is truly aware of our human qualities, but we neglect to understand that first and foremost that we are spirits housed in a body. We must cultivate our inner qualities and nourish the spirit. As the Bible states, "Man does not live by bread alone but by every word that proceeds out of the mouth of the Lord."

It is the constraints that we impose upon ourselves not those that are apparent, but those constraints that are self-imposed. As author Eric Butterworth states:, "Although we are limited in the human realm, we have unlimited potential in the mind of Christ." As your uncle, I want you to know that I too am growing and working to figure this life out that God has given me. Take it one day at a time, and remember that you are not alone.

      Be grateful.
      Love, Uncle Calvin

Dear Antoine
April 7, 2006

I certainly was glad to hear from you. There isn't a day that goes by that my thoughts are not on you. I took such delight in receiving your letter, and in a sense, it was like having you right in my presence. That is one thing about writing someone a letter. It affords one an opportunity to add a personal touch or flavor to a situation. Again, it reminds me of the frequent one-on-one sessions that we had together.

I must agree you are more like a son to me than a nephew in certain respects. I feel a kinship with you that is more of a spiritual connection, especially during your extended stay with us. I know that your presence here served both of us well on many levels. It was as if the Lord brought us together in response to certain needs we both had at the time. The more you lean on the Lord and rely on him and his ways, the better off we are.

At this juncture in my life, there isn't a day that goes by that my thoughts are not on serving the Lord. I am more focused on having a Christ-centered life. I know beyond a shadow of doubt that God is my inexhaustible supply. I truly can attest to the fact that I have come this far by faith. I owe everything that I am to the Lord. I know that you must be going through a lot right now. But be ever so mindful that God is everywhere. Also trust in the Lord with all your might, and you can't go wrong.

Life is full of so many toils and snares till it becomes imperative that we develop a personal relationship with God.

Again, like I told you before, you're going through something but remember as Caleb a young child said in Sunday Service, a profound statement at that: "I am glad that the Lord got my back." You know the Lord is real and that he is a wonder in your life.

With all the changes that I have gone through and continue to experience, it is only through the grace of God that I am able to do what I do. I truly am grateful for all those who have assisted me throughout my journey. I must admit that I had assistance every step of the way from many and diverse sources. Over the years, I have come to realize the value of what is meant by the statement that we all have a designated path to follow. A path that was predestined for us to follow and the Lord is present at every turn.

God has a way of getting our undivided attention; everything in the universe is in divine order, and again, he has a designated path for us to follow. As I told you at our last meeting, I confided in you something that I really regard as privileged information. It is a rarity that I disclose the fact that I had a nervous breakdown as they often say in layman terminology. Essentially, I was experiencing a lot of interpersonal difficulty, and I didn't know how to handle it.

Like you, I experienced a crisis and didn't know how to handle it. But unlike you, I didn't know the Lord or the significance of prayer when I was sitting around worrying. I should have been praying or in someone's church. My father and I were not communicating, and I didn't know how to share my feelings with others. Confronted with competing interests, my commitment to school and to my family/child (baby mama drama), I was insecure and couldn't handle it.

I was trying to prove to myself and to others that I could handle the situation of a family and school. My father and I were estranged at a time when I really needed him and was emotionally dependent on him. I didn't want my mother to get caught up in my conflictual relationship with my father. It never occurred to me that they were discussing the matter anyway. It was just something about my father telling me that I was going to fail at a time when I was so dependent on him and needed his support. It rubbed me the wrong way; I felt crushed, and I just tuned him out.

Excluding my father was not the best thing to do, but it seemed like it at the time. But hey I was young, and I really didn't know what I was doing. As you can see, not only do I like to talk at length, but I also can be rather expansive when I write. For a person who likes to write, I should write more often. But getting back to my point, I am going at length in discussing the matter. This really is a teaching moment for me to testify to the goodness of God. The Lord has truly been a watchman on the wall. When I wasn't a good steward over my affairs, the Lord was. God truly is a good God all the time. The Bible states it in such plain terms: "If it wasn't for the Lord on my side where I would be?"

I truly can attest to the fact that I have come this far by the grace of God. At an earlier phase in my life, I was essentially stumbling through life. I had an idealistic philosophical vantage point. Being witty is one thing, but knowing the Lord was truly another level all together. But God in his infinite mercy revealed himself to me in so many ways, sometimes pronounced and sometimes subtle ways. People have assisted me in my life every step of the way. Essentially, there is a season and a reason for everyone who enters your life.

There are some who enter for a fleeting moment, such as a chance occurrence at a bus stop or some for a more extended period but brief in the continuum of duration. Then there are those who are there for a lifetime. But in each case their impact on you extends beyond the constraints of time and can have a very profound impact on your well-being.

With the great mind that you have and what God has to offer you, I anticipate great things from you. I used to say with what I have to offer you, but now it is apparent to me that God truly has a great need for your services. Despite appearances, the Lord has found favor in you. Be aware that for those whom he calls he qualifies. You have been set apart for a great assignment. When they say that God's ways are not like our ways, he had situations like this in mind. We have defining moments in our life such that can cause us to question God. Remember that our faith affords us an opportunity to triumph during times of trouble. There are events that bring us to our knees. But mindful that when life brings you down to your knees, that's the perfect time to pray. When God has need of our services, he has a way of getting our undivided attention.

In closing, there is a lot more I would like to say, but it would take an even more extended letter to address those concerns.

YOU truly are in a good position to master yourself and come into an understanding of realizing your Spiritual Awakening. Be ever so mindful of the scripture: "Greater is he that is in you than he that is in the world." Trust in the Lord, and you can't go wrong, and remember wherever you are God is. Keep on climbing, and may God invoke his blessings on you.

Thank God all is well,

Love, Uncle Calvin

My Dad's Birthday
April 29, 2007

Dear Dad,

I know you are gone, and it has been quite a while, but I still feel your presence. Oftentimes, I am aware of you and know that your spirit is still in the midst. I look at my sons, and I can see your features in a very pronounced way. There are also times when I think of your experiences as a father, husband, provider, and mediator as well as your own interpersonal drama you had to contend with. As a matter of fact, I come to appreciate you and your journey many times over as I make my journey through life. Proverbially speaking, it is when you walk in another person's moccasins that can you appreciate them.

It has been nearly fourteen years since your demise, but I think of you so strongly at times and refer to you as a point of contact. When I engage in thought-provoking dialogue with my elders, I begin to think it would be nice if you were still around. It is then that I am mindful that the universe wants me to be in touch with you. It is not unusual that I still have a need to commune with you; as a matter of fact, it is incumbent of me that I do share with you. Even as I write, it is apparent that we shared a bond that transcends time and space.

You once referred to me as the apple of your eye to remind me of how valuable I am to you, and as a father of five children while all my children are important to me, they each play a unique and distinct part in my life.

On a continuum, as you can concur, your children assume different roles at different times of your life. In my youth, as a young parent, my daughters helped me stay anchored and directed my path in so many ways. I was always mindful of the father-daughter construct I conveyed to them.

Essentially, there is a lot of energy as parents that we transfer onto our children, and they in turn transfer a lot of energy unto us. It is a circular issue to say the least. As a seasoned father, this is an open letter to all fathers. As it often stated, fathers are unsung heroes of today. Yes, you do have athletes and entertainers, but what about the guy who gets up and goes to work and provides for his family?

There were many times when I didn't understand my father and things that he insisted upon, but now my children look at me in the same perplexed way. I hear you, but I don't understand you. My father insisted that I stay on the stoop/porch just as I requested from my children. I must admit I was a very obedient child, and I did feel like my parents smothered me, especially my father.

But I must borrow from the words of Horace Silver's song for my father: "if there was ever a man that was generous gracious and good, it was my dad." He sacrificed a lot to provide for his family. We had our moments, and at the birth of my first child, we grew estranged from one another. From that estrangement and the period preceding his death, shortly after my marriage, he asked my wife for a grandson. You know God in his wisdom and mercy gave him his wish; a dying man was granted his wish, and it came in the form of my son Elijah.

I am truly grateful to my dad. He is my hero. I am who I am in large measure because of my dad.

I look at my dad differently beyond the estrangement. When I reflect on him, the greater part of me looks at what he did and what he aspired to achieve. A phrase that he often quoted has become my quote: "I may not be the man that I want to be, but I thank God that I am not the man that I was."

Love you, Dad.

A Letter to My Brother

Dear William

At the expense of sounding cliché, you are gone but not forgotten. I don't know if your demise was so recent or the fact that your words still resonate throughout my being. I know you really were preparing me for your journey into the marvelous light. You were not only praising me for my assistance but were encouraging me to exemplify as well as embrace the role that God had ordained for me to follow.

True to form, you have always been my trusted friend and confidante down through the years. I am ever so mindful that during my youth you encouraged me to become a lawyer. During one of our late-night discourses, you shared career aspirations that you had, and you realized that as a lawyer I would be an asset to you should any misfortune befall you, being the enterprising individual that you were. As a lawyer, one day I would be governor as well, making my position even more beneficial to you.

Well dear brother, from the late-night diatribe, I began my career path and concurrently so did you. As fate would have it, God had other plans for both of us. Amazingly, both our paths were laden with many toils and snares that ultimately aided us in our spiritual awakening. For it would give us a keen insight into the human condition and realization that it was the grace of God that allowed us to circumvent destruction not only physical but our spiritual integrity.

I want you to know that God had already predestined us for greatness and had decreed a manner for us to give him Glory. He had already given us gifts and talents that exceeded anything that we acquire from man. The experiences brought us closer to God and the realization that the Lord would make a way of escape for us. Where a door is closed, a window is opened. As you would often say, lean on the Lord and not your own understanding. I will never forget all that I learned from you and what I continue to discover within the words of wisdom you shared.

Your Brother,
Calvin

Dear Nip

I was just thinking about you, as I often do, and to quote a phrase that you used many years ago: "all goodbyes are not gone." Although you are not here, I can still feel your presence. Now is the time when I could really benefit from our late-night sessions of meaningful dialogue where we shared our dreams and aspirations. I like to talk, but I enjoy being in a contemplative mode as well.

Most times, I find myself in a contemplative mode focused on spiritual matters and my relationship with God and how I can best serve him. Spiritual matters are spiritually discerned. God is Spirit, and we must worship him in Spirit and Truth. I appreciate your parting words to me: start making fuller use of my gift. People expect a lot out of me; it is time for me to expect more out of myself. As we have been taught to go out on location and find God for ourselves.

We must embrace our divinity unabated. To accept our divinity and live accordingly to realize our oneness with God. As Jesus stated, the father and I are one. We have the very attributes of God. We are made in the image and likeness of God.

Now, I know this is more than just verbiage or idle words. It sounds good, but this can be a way of life. As it is written, be not conformed to this world but transformed by the renewal of your mind. As you would say, dear brother, it is all about the way that you think. As the Bible states, as a man thinks in his heart so is he. You encouraged me to stop doubting myself and being afraid and to step out on faith. I can do all things through Christ who strengthens me. Christ is the knowledge and wisdom of God unto salvation. Christ is the mind of God individualized. We are limited in the human realm, but we have unlimited potential in the divine. We are spirits housed in a body; we are God's manifestation here on earth.

We both had interesting journeys in life, we went through our own respective school of hard knots, and subsequently we went on to a path of enlightenment. As time went by, we both graduated to a higher consciousness. When I look back, I come to realize that God had a plan for both of us to follow and ultimately, we both existed in a complimentary path. We both came to understand and appreciate one another, and it all stems from our early experiences with one another.

Fortunately, one of us is still here to both live and tell our story. Just as I saw you as an admirable character in your youth, I found you even more admirable in your later years. Just like you pursued your years of foolishness and folly with so much passion, you put just as much passion into your Spiritual Awakening. Like yourself, my spiritual awakening manifested itself later in my life. In both cases, it proved to be advantageous to ourselves and others. Again, I am grateful to you.

God bless you in the Spirit World.

You understood me and appreciated me at times when I didn't have an inclination of who I was or whose I was. When people know you and appreciate you throughout your good points and not so good points, you truly have found a friend. I enjoy you even though you're not here in the body. I must commend you for the role and impact that you have had on my life. As scholarly and astute as we both were becoming as students of the word, it was just a matter of time before we both blossomed.

Your presence transcends time and space. As you would often state, the Spirit never dies; you keep a person alive by invoking their name. I am still conscious of your spirit. I just took the time to acknowledge you.

Dear Wesley
May 20, 2010

There isn't a day that goes by that I don't share a thought or tear about you. I am still aware of your presence and the impact that you had on my life. We often stated that we were twins even though our birthdays were fourteen months apart. We were often referred to as big baby and little baby. Our bond was a little different than the other siblings; we had our own pact to look out for one another.

Your demise/suicide takes on a certain meaning to me. I wish you would have said something to me. You tried to, but you couldn't verbalize it to me. I felt something was going to happen to you; you had a sense of gloom and desperation in your eyes. You tried to mask it with laughter and seemingly joy, but it was all a façade, the "tears of a clown."

Once before, you asked me why I didn't try to help you, and I responded that I did, but you were not receptive to it. As a matter of fact, you would make mockery of it and dismiss it or deny that there was a problem. But you and I were really joined at the hip; we had our own internal dialogue, and even though we traveled in different circles, we were still there for one another.

Again, you are not here now, but I am still aware of your presence and the profound impact you have on my life. Even though you had a sense of courage that was reckless and defiant at times, you were the one who was willing to take a leap of faith. Contrasted with myself, I tended to be quiet and reserved and pursued things in a cautionary matter. With that in mind, you could say we were a study of two contrasted spirits.

Most of the fights that I had were because of you, but the biggest battle that I would have, you were there for me every step of the way. The battle in the mind proved to be my most formidable foe. The battle brought tears to my dad; I never saw him consumed with so much grief. My dad introduced me to the power of prayer and assured me that everything would be all right. Also, later, you emphatically told me when I was in a state hospital that I deserved better, and you assured me that I would be all right.

Years later, when you experienced your own battle in your mind, I desired to give you what you gave me. As the battle began to unfold, you resisted my intervention and ultimately the battle proved to be stronger than both of us. The factors that influenced my battle are that I humbled myself and in contrast you tried to defy it.

Worth noting is that although we were an interesting contrast, we could still work together on a certain level, but because you had become increasingly more complicated, the contrasting styles were causing us to become more distant. Our opposing lifestyles and distinct priorities were beginning to take a toll on our relationship, causing us to be worlds apart at a time when we both needed one another.

Even though we were apart, my thoughts and prayers were for you, but I wish that I would have been able to reach you, and

I deeply regret that I could not be there for you. As I capture the moments leading up to your death, it is clear what your intentions were. I know you are in the Spirit, but I must ask for your forgiveness because I forgive you, and I ask God to forgive you as well. I love you dearly, and may God have mercy on your soul.

                        Love you always,
                        Calvin

Dear Antoine
December 10, 2010

Hold on and know that your deliverance shall come. Often when we think of deliverance, we equate that with some hostile force or forces outside of us. But to the contrary, the deliverance is best understood from the hostile force or forces that reside within our mind. As they say, the battle is in our mind and how we tend to internalize our struggle. It is often said that just before we experience a change or breakthrough, we must contend with our biggest obstacle. Just before relief, there is the distress.

I like to talk to you about my early struggles in life because those trials and tribulations brought forth my greatest lessons about life and living. Now I am going there for a reason; there is still some pain connected to these experiences, and I remember talking to a doctor about these events, and in talking about these things, I remember conjuring the same emotions and reliving that experience. The year of 1979 proved to be one of turbulence for me; from the beginning to the ending, it seemed like I had the Midas Touch in reverse. Instead of everything I touched turning to gold, it literally turned to waste. I was flunking out of school, didn't have a love life or love interest, and was tired of the dating scene.

Nor was I working. I had launched a business venture with Abdul that wasn't going well. I was still grieving over the death of my mother. Now here is where everything goes from bad to worse.

I was involved with a therapist that I didn't like. Had an illness that I didn't like or accept. On medication that I didn't like or accept. My family dynamics were becoming too difficult. My support system was fragile, fragmented, and dysfunctional to say the least. Speaking of that reverse Midas Touch, I stopped taking my medication. All this proved to be a recipe for disaster.

Little did I know all these events would become a way of inspiring and teaching countless others. Ultimately, I had another breakdown that should not come as a surprise considering the preceding variables. Again, this was not a good year for me. When they say can things get worst, well they didn't have to, but in my case, they did. I am telling these things to you for a reason, and I am doing my best to be brutally honest with you.

My goal is to remind you that despite seemingly insurmountable conditions, you can prevail, just hold on and know that things can change for you.

In saying all that, I was in the hospital, came home on pass, and refused to go back. I am doing the best I can to make this both brief and concise and still be effective. In my teachings to the clients, I always emphasize the importance of medication compliance with the emphasis and understanding that they are aware that they have a chemical imbalance. Now I had to return to the hospital to have my meds adjusted. At this point, this was my second hospitalization. Be mindful I had yet to have remission of the symptoms, and I was still out of it.

Therefore, exhibiting poor judgment, I walked away from this hospitalization. Essentially, I escaped. After escaping, I eventually had to be committed to a state hospital against my will, and my father and others tried to convince me to go back in to treatment, but I was too out of it to understand that there were trying to help me. I am going at length to encourage you to be fully aware that even when it doesn't seem like it, there is a force or forces that are watching over you, so continue to hold on.

I spent approximately 60 days in the hospital. It was while I was there that I began to realize how fortunate I was despite prevailing conditions. In the months preceding that, I was essentially in a country club setting where I received the best of care and fabulous food in a clean and sanitary environment. During this hospitalization, I saw some stuff there and was subjected to very insensitive individuals more so the staff that took their frustrations out on the patients. But amid all that, it proved to be my turning point.

You may ask was I bitter about the experience, and my answer would be, no, I wasn't. I did not start my entry into psychology right away, but eventually I did, and that pursuit was fueled by that experience. The social worker at the time told me it was time for me to go home, but I told her I wasn't sure. She, however, gave me encouraging words and told me again it was time to go.

As a reminder to myself, your father came and visited me and pleaded with me to get myself together, that I deserved better. My father only came to see me once.

My uncle Bishop never did come to see me like he did when I was in the hospital the first time. But I am indebted to Nettie, for she was my right hand upon my reentry into society. She was an asset to me. I must give honor to all those who made it possible for me to become the person that I am today. Now I wasn't angry, but my spirits were broken, and I was depressed. My daughters I must make mention of because they were also a source of inspiration to me. I didn't know how it was going to happen, but I knew something had to happen. At this moment, I am writing this to remind you to hold on and stay encouraged, or am I writing this a remainder to myself to hold on and to stay encourage. I really know that we both need some encouragement right about now.

With that in mind, let me continue. Upon coming home, I was very low in spirits, and people in later years asked me how I could put up with so much stuff from my family, especially Wesley. Well, when I came home at that point, I needed all the help I could get and more. Your father was so patient and compassionate with me. My father did the best he could and the best he knew how to do.

It was difficult for me, but it was just as difficult for him.

The first time it happened to me your uncle Abdul told me he had never seen my father so worried. I was so angry at my father for not being there at that point. I always lashed out at him just like Josh,. Instead of talking to him, I went from the passive child to one who was very confrontational and hostile more so toward him than anyone else. This was not how I acted after the second episode; I am referring to the first episode.

The second time around proved to be a humbling experience. Your father and Nettie were two key players for me early on. Nettie was instrumental in me obtaining and maintaining my employment at Harper Hospital. I filled out the application in Nov. 1979. You know that was the only application I filled out at that time, and I didn't think any more about it. My father had plans to get married that following April, and he wanted me to be okay and to be able to handle myself. I told him I would be okay.

Also, I had applied for Social Security Disability, which my father was opposed to. He felt I should get a job. When they denied me that option again, he told me to get a job and do something more with myself. I saw my father pray for me, and he did shed tears on more than one occasion. Yes, he did raise some hell in typical Bill Thompson fashion, but all these things were done out of love. He didn't give up on me, and I am not giving up on you (smile!). Again, I am trying to be clear and concise, but as you can see, I need to be inspired as well, and the more I write, the better I feel.

You know how I feel about you, son. I just wish I could be of more assistance to you on many levels. You're more like a son to me, and you remind of how I felt and still feel toward my beloved uncle Bishop. I understand the comment that you made about your mother and how she felt about my relationship with you. My father and I had a special relationship, but my relationship with my uncle was on another level; he was there for me and understood what my needs were, and for that I will always be indebted to him.

Likewise, I have the same sentiments for your dad. I know what he became, but I know what he was to me. When I came home, he welcomed me, helped me get back on my feet in a nonjudgmental and nurturing manner that was instrumental in my wellness—the kind of things brothers do for one another. What else can I say? It speaks for itself. I know I have said a lot, but there is a lot that needs to be said about matters of this nature. This is such a sensitive topic for me, but for whatever the reason, you and I both have a need. Hopefully, we will both feel better after this session of sharing and caring.

The Transformation

My Next Move

As it is so often stated, this is the first day of the rest of your life. With that in mind, let this be a new beginning for me. If I have life in my body, I still have a chance. I must admit I pray to God every day that he allows me to be delivered from an adversarial relationship that I have with myself. As much time and energy that I devote to the salvation of others, I need to devote more attention to my own needs.

It is nice to encourage others and remind them of the enormous gifts and talents they have embedded in them. Shall I also remind myself of the hidden jewels that I have embedded within myself? People always tell me how much they admire or respect my talents; isn't it time for me to start accepting my blessings as well? Have I allowed myself to be so sidelined by fear and doubt that I foster and adversarial relationship with myself?

I know that it is quite common for people to be limited more so by elements within them rather than external factors. We often undermine ourselves and fail to realize that our real greatness resides within us. As the Bible states, "Greater is that which resides within us than that which in the world." Our resource is readily available, waiting for us to make full use of it. The spirit of almighty God resides within us all.

God made us in his image and likeness and breathed into the nostrils of man and made him a living soul. We are a form of God, and as such, I have the very attributes of God. We must become more mindful of who we are in the eyesight of God and the enormous potential that we have from the vantage point of the creator.

We tend to marginalize and minimize our existence, being more preoccupied with our limitations. In the human realm, we do have limited potential, but in the divine mind of Christ, our potential is unlimited. Jesus stated, "Great things have I done but greater things shall you do."

It is time for me to come into a fuller awareness of what it means to be a child of God. To let this mind be in me that was also in Christ Jesus. That we are transformed by the renewal of our mind. I must learn to lean on the Lord and not my own understanding, to trust in him with all my might. We come to the realization that there is no failure with God and that whatever we need God has it. We allow ourselves to be privy to the unlimited potential of the Christ mind. Christ is the particularization of the mind of God or the incarnation of God. We are representations of God manifested here on earth, spirits in earthly bodies.

We all are privy to the Christ consciousness; it is our birthright which God intends for us to come into awareness and to make full use of it. We can hear these things and see it manifest in others, but it is incumbent upon us to make it *our* reality. We must do like Jesus did. He personalized his relationship with God. He recognized the

I AM within him as he personalized his relationship with God when he said the Father and I are one. It is time for me to recognize a personal relationship with God.

The next move is to trust in the Lord and lean on him and not my own understanding, to live a life in accordance to his will. To live as if I am in the presence of God and to acknowledge him in all my endeavors. To not allow myself to operate in a manner that is separate from his will. To be in full compliance irrespective to and despite prevailing conditions. To remain steadfast in my convictions and not be swayed by doubt or fear. To recognize that I can do all things through Christ who strengthens me.

We are born with everything we need; it is up to us to make full use of our gifts and talents. God will give us the desires of our heart, for those things that we love that is God manifesting himself through us. Remember that your gifts and talents will make room for you. God has given me the ability to move and impact people's lives through the comforting words that I extend to them. Words do have healing power in them.

Being involved in the ministry as well as having extensive involvement in mental health has enhanced my interpersonal skills immensely. The two are one; either way, you are dealing with the mind.

It is time to accept my birthright in all its glory and be one with God, for he is the source from which I come. We do ourselves a grave disservice when we minimize ourselves when we are spiritual beings experiencing the human condition.

We must step out on faith; we have nothing to fear but fear itself. Peter was able to walk on water until he allowed his fears to overtake him. As Jesus stated, great things have I done, but greater things shall you do; let this mind be in you that was also in Christ

Jesus who being a form of God did not consider it robbery to be equal to God.

Again, I must come into an awareness of who I really am as a new creature in Christ. As the Bible states, "I can do all things through Christ who strengthens me."

Christ is the knowledge and wisdom of God unto salvation. I must begin to lean on the Lord and not my own understanding and trust in him with all my might. I have already been validated by the Lord; it is up to me to acknowledge and began to live a spirit-filled existence that is my birthright.

I am made in the image and likeness of God, and as such, I am a form of God. God breathed into the nostrils of man and made him a living soul. Be ever so mindful that breath and spirit come from the same root word; therefore, the spirit of the Lord resides within me—the Father and I are one. The natural order of things is to be on one accord with God. Again, lean on the Lord and not your own understanding and TRUST IN HIM WITH ALL YOUR MIGHT.

Manifesting My Desires

I can do all things through Christ who strengthens me.
Christ is the mind of God individualized, being mindful that we are the manifestation and expression of God. God is an awesome God, and so am I, for I am the personification of God. As Jesus said, the Father and I are one. I must focus on elevation and rise above the human eclipsiation of life and lean more on the divine mind of Christ, for Christ is the knowledge and wisdom of God unto Salvation.

I am both an asset as well as a liability to myself because of my level of thinking. For our thoughts are prophetic and self-fulfilling, for as a man thinks in his heart so is he. The very thoughts that we entertain manifest themselves as our actions. Thoughts are things and words materialize. We can create our world by the very thoughts that we entertain; it is essential that we come into a greater awareness of who we are and the greatness that resides within us.

We must rise above the constraints or limitations that we impose upon ourselves consciously or unconsciously. As it is stated, intentionally or unintentionally, one must think about what they think about. I must begin to speak things into existence.

Be mindful of this, although I am limited in the human realm, I have unlimited potential in the divine mind of Christ. Again, I must let myself be a new creature in Christ and accept my birthright as Jesus accepted his. Let this mind be in me that was also in Christ Jesus, who being a form of God did not consider it robbery to be equal with God; the difference was that of degree. We are made in the image and likeness of God.

God breathed into the nostrils of man and made him a living soul being mindful that breath and spirit come from the same root word; essentially, the spirit of the Lord is in you. It is written peace be still and know that I am God. In concise terms, it is stated that the God that is in me that allows me to achieve what I achieve, to do what I do as well as to be what I be. As it is written, the Father and I are one. Where one begins and the other ends, there is no distinction; we are inseparable. Being mindful that we have the very attributes of God, it is only natural that we should be one with God.

One must lean on the Lord and not their own understanding and to trust in him with all your might, and he will direct your path. It is written that we are not to be conformed to the world but to be transformed by the renewal of our mind. Unfortunately for most of us, myself included, we are already in the worldly mode; therefore, as Paul stated, daily I die not to the physical but the carnal mind or lower consciousness.

One must work on themselves daily and learn how to rise above the human distractions of life and lean on the divine mind of Christ. As it is written, Christ is the mind of God individualized. God is spirit, so one must worship him in spirit and truth. Being mindful that we are spiritual beings experiencing the human condition. God needed something to house his spirit in, so he made man. We are the manifestation and expression of God.

Again, it is our level and manner of thinking that makes a difference for us. The power of life and death exists in the tongues; one must focus on elevation and lend themselves to a higher consciousness despite the appearance of things.

Jesus stated if one believes a mountain can be moved, one can speak it into existence. One must be able to see beyond the immediacy of a crisis and see a point of resolution. One cannot be so overwhelmed by the appearance of things.

The scripture states "that the Lord will put no more on you than you can bear, for he will make the way of escape for the faithful." I must get out of the way and draw nearer to God and let him do his perfect work through me. My level of thinking must change. The problem cannot be changed at the same level of thinking that created it.

The critical periods in my life characterized as crises have brought forth some of my most creative thinking. For in the moment of distress, I had to go to the next level of thinking to create the atmosphere for change. The discomfort, distress, and disease were so overwhelming that opportunities availed themselves to me. Discomfort causes one to focus on relief; those creative juices get to flowing and resolution manifests itself. In my case, I began to have some serious talks with God, praising him and petitioning him every step of the way.

It is a mind thing; be not conformed to the world but ye transformed by the renewal of the mind. Be mindful that man's knowledge pales in comparison to God's. We have the very attributes of the Lord inside of us; therefore, it is only natural that we should live a life in accordance to his will irrespective to the appearance of things. We should operate as if we are in the very presence of God and furnish the life so that God can use us.

Our thoughts should agree with God always irrespective to the appearance of things we should know for a surety that God has the final say in all affairs. Doubting ourselves is one thing, but we should not doubt the sovereignty of the Lord.

I must focus on the irrefutable truth that God can deliver me from myself and be willing to submit to his will and not mine. For as it is so aptly put, my best thinking has created my own mess. For in the final analysis, this is a condition that I have brought on myself; therefore, the solution lies with me as well.

I must lean on the Lord and not my own understanding, and trust in him with all my might, and he will direct my path. For God is my inexhaustible vein of supply. Again, I must furnish the life so that God can use me and live as if I am in the very presence of the Lord.

When praises go up, blessings come down. I should have a mind that is stayed on the Lord or remain steadfast in my convictions and to trust the process. As Jesus stated: "He that believes in that which is in me great things have I done but greater thing shall you do."

There is a consciousness that resides within man that can liberate him from the self-imposed constraints that prevent him from reaching the lofty heights that he is endowed with. As Eric Butterworth states in *Discover the Power within You*, "Although we are limited in the human realm we have unlimited potential in the divine mind of Christ." It is important, as Lord Shaffer would say, that we " must rise above the human eclipsiation of life and lean more on the divine mind of Christ."

We can do all things through Christ that strengthens us. One must focus on elevation and lift their mind. It is hard when one is consumed with distress, disease, or problems.

One must let their faith be bigger than their problems. Problems cannot be solved at the same level of thinking that created them. We have the very attributes of the Lord inside of us. Be mindful that we are made in the image and likeness of God.

Being that we are a form of God, we are to operate in the manner and similitude of God. We are to act as Jesus did and be one with God and to demonstrate the Christ consciousness, for to be Christ like is to be Godlike. WE ARE TO BE ON ONE ACCORD WITH GOD AT ALL TIMES FOR THAT IS HIS EXPECTATION OF US.

For God expects more out of us than what he is getting; he wants us to keep his commandments and to live a full and abundant life. For the Lord made us in the best of molds, a little lower than the angels. He knows what we are made of, and he wants us to come into a realization of which we are in his eyesight and to live accordingly.

We are instructed to not be conformed to the world but to be transformed by the renewal of our mind. Lest we forget that Christ is the mind of God individualized. We are the manifestation and expression of God. Therefore, it is only natural that we should live in accordance to his will and exhibit his consciousness unabated.

Our oneness with the Lord is the key to our salvation; we must honor the will of the Lord and live a spirit-filled existence. It is our separation from the Lord that is the root of our problem.

We suffer needlessly when we don't honor the Lord or the God that is in us.

Leaving

Sometimes loving someone is not enough. The difficulties in a marriage put you in the dubious position of contending with differences that are not reconcilable. Ours was a household that had been too divided for too long.

I did not want to leave my family, but I felt compelled to do so and had been feeling that way for years. I had become consumed with grief and couldn't shake these feelings.

There were challenges that my wife and I had to contend with that just were bigger than our love. Like it is often stated, love is not enough. Again, it was a regrettable but necessary move.

The move recaptures the sentiments of when I left my family of origin on Hecla; the players are different, but the synopsis was the same. In both cases, I became worn and weary of my family dynamics. We had ceased to be a vibrant and endearing family.

We have become too conflictual and distant from one another. In the case of me and my wife, we both acknowledged our despondency. The issues with our son Joshua were an added ongoing issue that should have been dealt with earlier.

Having a blended family is not easy, and it wasn't easy for us. This was not the way we started out, but we got off track, and we were having difficulty getting back on track.

What made both situations so difficult is that we were fighting against one another with no end in sight. We were suffering needlessly because we were without a vision. We were a house divided on key principles, going against everything that I stood for.

As in the case of Hecla, my tenure there was over. I didn't fit into that way of thinking. My wife and I were so different and not only did our marriage suffer but so did our family constellation. This was not the family life that I envisioned for us. When we married one another, we really fell short of our objective.

There is no doubt we both deserved better from one another, and it just wasn't practical to go through the motions of an estranged relationship and the grievous state of our family. We all were operating outside of the will of the creator, allowing ourselves to conduct our affairs in a manner that was not consistent with a Godly nature. Being consumed with rage and contempt toward one another, these are not the ingredients of a loving home.

The family that prays together stays together; it doesn't state that the family that preys on one another prevails over one another. We were undermining one another and promoting a hostile environment. It was becoming increasingly difficult for me to function in my home. It was not the life that I envisioned for myself. If it was difficult for me, then it was just as difficult for the entire family. Really, is that the way to live? I would have to say emphatically no.

WE SHOULD HAVE BROUGHT THE BEST OUT OF ONE ANOTHER INSTEAD OF THE WORST. When so much time and energy is put on being right, at some point it becomes a moot point. Everyone standing their ground in a maladapted way becomes a recipe for disaster. One could very well be right, but one's presentation could negate their point. In each other's face trying to prove a point. What is the point? Losing respect for one another and disrespecting yourself. How long do you think God is going to just sit back and allow one to self-destruct in that matter?

I know that the Bible says that one should honor thy mother and father so that your day will be long and prosperous. But reference is also made to the fact that parents should not provoke their children to anger. At what point then does it become appropriate that one should not consider the possibility to settle their disputes with their adversaries? Being mindful that the adversary can be you because of the anger that we have can become displaced or misdirected at others.

One must be cognizant of the things that they do intentionally or unintentionally. We can harbor such ill feelings toward someone or something that we fail to be aware of how we come across to others. We emit a certain vibration or tendency before we act on them and others pick up on our vibrations or tendencies before we act on them. We are encouraged to acknowledge God's presence in everything and everyone.

We are encouraged to live as if we are in the very presence of God and to conduct our affairs and don't compartmentalize or exclude him from the equation.

My concern at this point, is although I am a minister and student of the word and expound and exhibit it elsewhere, it was not evident in my home. I was not happy or joyful in that setting. Not only was I distant or disconnected from my children, but I was becoming more disconnected from my wife as well. It was obvious that something was wrong, but nothing was being done about it. I wasn't so inclined to do a lot as I had been so inclined to do in the early years of our relationship.

One can always talk about how we used to be, but one must give as much attention to the way that we are as well. One must take inventory to be more precise. One must take fearless inventory of themselves as well. It does take two to tangle; one cannot be in this battle by themselves. Had I gotten to know my wife before I came to know her, we might have stood a better chance or considered other options. Even more so, like so many couples, we should have addressed a lot of our issues in a better manner as opposed to pointing the finger at one another.

I am sure, like countless others, we could have been more understanding of one another and made allowances for each other's personal growth and development. After all you can't raise someone at best you may be able to influence them and motivate them to change. Speaking of change, it's important to be mindful of the changes that occurred during our relationships.

As strong of an affinity we both had for marijuana and cigarettes, we both stopped that. Worth noting is that I began to take better care of my health and get regular checkups. From a preventive perspective, that is always an asset.

In the realm of spiritual matters, my public speaking and ministry took off, something I expressed a desire to do prior to our marriage. Even more, just as Mother Woods predicted, I would have sons and one would be just like me. I must admit the marriage hasn't been all bad. We just got off the path and forgot our way like so many couples. We stopped giving the part of ourselves that made it work; our differences and our dislikes became the focal point not the fact that we were a force when we were together.

As I said from the outset, we had become consumed with grief, and we couldn't shake those feelings. We admitted something was wrong, but neither one of us was making or taking the initiative to change the direction of things, and that was a bad sign. Things were going from bad to worst; we were not encouraged by one another. We both were operating from a low frequency, and it was showing up in other areas of our life.

Yes, I chose Lela as my wife because despite things at least she was consistent, she would be there. Yes, there was room for improvement, and I was willing to do the work and so was she. What else could explain the extended time together? Twenty-four years is a long time to be together. All that we went through, it was only a matter of time that we experienced the proverbial straw that broke the camel's back. Stuff happens, and it just so happened that stuff happened to us, but we must keep it moving like most couples. Our relationship is no different.

Regardless to what others say or think, we did the best we knew how, and that is all that God asks of us. We were good for each other, and we accomplished what we needed to accomplish in the appointed time that we were together. I trust that we have a better relationship with ourselves because we had one another. I think about the high points as well as the low points in our relationship. When it was good, it was good. When it wasn't so good, we dealt with that as well. As it is said, no one knows what goes on behind closed doors; the pact that couples make to prevail and contend with adversity despite themselves or their circumstances.

There is a code of conduct that couples contend with that has its own distinct flavor or as one would say it's complicated to others but we have an understanding because it works for us. There is a lot of unspoken language that goes on a relationship that others are not privy to, but couples know what they know, and they respond accordingly. It is hard to explain, but this is the wing nut that has allowed for us to endure the obstacles and seemingly mountainous situations that seemed insurmountable but somehow, we made it. Situations that made us stronger and wiser, things that made God smile when he was well pleased with us and what we aspired to achieve.

A quarter of a century is a long time to be with someone, but really that person will always be with you because you both figure into each other's personal growth and development.

You watched each other blossom on each other's watch and the omnipresence of all mighty God. God provides for the lilies of the field and keeps his eye on the sparrow, so I know that he watches over me. God knew what he was doing when he gave man a helpmate in the form of a wife. For as it is decreed that the two of you are to be twain and cling to one another as we were instructed to not let any third party get in the way of our relationship.

We both must take the responsibility for the issues that we allowed to get in the way of our relationship. It might have been something as simple as Mother Woods asking me in the period preceding her death did we encourage one another. Initially, I said yes, but on reflection, I said no. If your spouse is not your number one fan, then you must look at why they're not. This is where you ask yourself some difficult questions about whether or not your actions are encouraging to them. Some things are circular by nature. If we are honest, we feed off one another, and we reap what we sow in relationships.

Emphatically, we did enjoy one another on some level at some point in time. Even with the challenges we experienced, we still held on to one another. We just ran out of gas and stopped encouraging one another and started taking one another for granted. If we would have confronted each other and dealt with each other in a more comprehensive manner, chances are we would be together now. Too much was going on that we should have nipped in the bud before it started to define our relationship.

WE HAD OUR TIME TOGETHER, AND WE ACCOMPLISHED WHAT WE WERE INTENDED TO OR NEEDED TO ACCOMPLISH AT THIS JUNCTURE. WE MUST PART COMPANY ON AMICABLE TERMS AND BE THE BEST THAT WE CAN BE FOR EACH OTHER NOW.

There is no need to be adversaries currently; we deserve more out of one another than that. After all, we shared each other's life experience for a quarter of century, and it is not unusual for couples to grow distant from one another even after a lengthy time together. It would be more regrettable to have deep-rooted animosity toward another I cannot say that is the case for me. I just felt that we had outgrown one another and our differences were just that we were so different and had been from the start.

They say opposites attract and make for good relationships, but any good relationship is only as good as the couple and how they mesh together. In our relationship, there was just too much division, and we did not work together like we should have. I told Mother Woods about how different we were and how concerned I was about it, and she tried to give us assurance that it would be okay.

We came together at a time when we both needed someone to fill the void in our life, and Mother Woods predicted that I was going to get married soon, and lo and behold, Lela was the one I was smitten by. There were other prospects, but she was the one I chose. But I must admit there was a little more to it than that. I had my own challenges at the time. I wanted something more than just convenience.

Another factor was that I still was smoking marijuana at the time, and I wasn't ready to relinquish that habit, and I smoked cigarettes as well, two strikes against me in an increasing health conscious environment some of the women whom I was around did not even know of those habits. So, when I met Lela, and she liked to smoke marijuana, that made it convenient to do so. Worth noting, when it was time to stop, her presence figured into the process as well, and for that, I will be eternally grateful.

Another point worth mentioning is my father came over to my apartment and commented something to me in passing; he suggested to me that I should marry a younger woman, so I could have some more children. After Lela and I married, he came over to the house when the two of them were alone, and he asked her to have a grandson for him. Never mind the fact that at this juncture he had many grandchildren and great-grandchildren inclusive. I have my theory on why he made that request of my wife for a child on more than one level.

Shortly after we were married, my father had to have a heart bypass surgery, and within a year, he was diagnosed with colon cancer, which he eventually succumbed to. Having my wife proved to be a blessing to me in helping me deal with my father's transition.

Leaving someone is never easy, but for you to go to the next dimension of who you are, it is imperative that one draw the proverbial line in the sand. Love is a peculiar entity at times when you have become more attached to one another and stop extending the care and attention to one another as you should or could.

Church Life

Where are all the people, or a funny thing happened while I was on my way to church.

Not to make a mockery of things, but doesn't it seem that in a time when there is an urgent need for souls to be saved that people are conspicuously absent from houses of worship? There is a noticeable absence of people from fellowshipping together these days. The houses of worship are filled with more women than men, and where I go to worship, on a good day, there may be 20 people in attendance. Rarely do we average 40 people in attendance.

Now mind you when there are special events, there has been standing room only. But as a rule, the attendance on most Sundays is not that much. Where the folks are on the other Sundays your guess is as good as mine. I am sure the reasons can be as varied as the number of members that we have. A point of interest is that in our case a major reason for the 20 faithful attendants is their allegiance to the leader of the organization.

An allegiance to a leader is one thing, but an allegiance to the Lord should be your vested interest. The message should exceed the messenger; we should not be so mesmerized by the messenger that we lose perspective on things. In a day of sophisticated telecommunications and spin doctors, it is easy to get caught up in the hype and sensationalism. But one must make a concerted effort to distinguish themselves.

In a day in which we are inundated with idolatry and vain pursuits, one must know with a surety who they are and whose they are. The churches of today must recognize and distinguish themselves from an emerging theme of today of being likened to a wolf in sheep's clothing. When our spiritual leaders don their garbs, they must know who they are in the eyesight of God and not have their own agenda separate from God.

We live in a day whether we want to or not where things are becoming more transparent; those who are not living in accordance with the rules of proper engagement are being revealed as such. The need for integrity is so great that for all practical purposes, God's words are not coming back void of understanding. God is raising up a nation that will obey him.

Hold on, I encourage you. Despite appearances, we are moving in the direction that God wants us to go before it is over with. People will come into a greater awareness of what their role is in the eyesight of God and start living accordingly.

Living a life separate from God is the root of our problems and even more so is having wavering commitment to God. We cannot serve two masters, for we cannot be in the church and the world.

Our allegiance is to the Lord irrespective to what is going on. We are to hold on to his unchanging hands to know for a fact that he has a ram in the bush for the faithful. God made us in his image and likeness; therefore, we have to give homage to him and keep his commandments. As the Bible states, we are to honor our parents so that our days are long and prosperous. Again, we are instructed to keep God's commandments and live. To furnish our lives so God can use us. Be mindful that God cannot live in an unclean vessel. We cannot be wavering or double-minded, for as the Bible states, a double-minded person is unstable in all their ways.

We must live a life and be mindful of the omnipresence of God and live accordingly with the full understanding that wherever we are, God is fully aware of our actions always. We can run, but we can't hide from God. There is no mountain too high or river too wide or valley too low to get away from God, for God is in every vacant place. Wherever we are, God is.

The honorable thing for us to do is to be available so God can use us. It is not just the building that we should give homage to. First and foremost, we are the embodiment of the church. As a child of God, we are to represent God wherever we go and let that Good Spirit guide our path and to be mindful of our duty to God and give God the glory in everything we do. Don't do anything that is contrary to the will of God.

Once again, if we want to fill these churches up, start being a testimony to the goodness of God and being a willing participant in his kingdom building and not a reluctant warrior. As one song so eloquently puts it: "this little light of yours let it shine wherever you go." We must be positive role models and exemplify the consciousness of what a Christian is.

As a Christian, we are a separate and distinct entity in the scheme of things. There should be a mark distinction between those who are in the world and those who are not.

Manifestation

We are God's manifestation and expression here on earth. Essentially, we are spirits housed in a body, a form of God. Man was given dominion over all of God's creation and the ability to rule in a manner that is pleasing to God. It is important that we carry ourselves in such a way that reflects his majesty and grace while striving to bring out the best in one another. The best way we can do this is by loving the Lord with all our might and learning to love our neighbor as ourselves. The operative condition for all humanity is to love others, even in adversarial relationship. Although it can be challenging to show compassion in contemptuous situations to others, for myself included, it is a practice that we must learn to master.

As Christians, we have an enormous responsibility to one another; we must be in full compliance with the word of God always. Being mindful that we are set apart for a reason. This is not something that we give lip service to; no, this a way of life. We have come into awareness that Christ is a consciousness; it is the mind of God individualized.

When Jesus said that the Father and I are one, he was acknowledging that he and the Father were inseparable. That he was on one accord with God despite anything to the contrary he remained steadfast in his convictions.

As a child of God, we have an unyielding faith and know the value of holding on to God's unchanging hands. We recognize the God in us and give him the glory and shun the very presence of evil or doing anything that is contrary to the will of God.

With that in mind, a funny thing happened to me on the way to church. It became clear that God's message was timeless and relevant to those who would receive it. As Jesus said, the message was for those that have eyes to see and ears to hear. I am grateful that God gave me a sense of discernment to understand the relevance of being a faithful and an obedient servant.

The Bible states, fail not to assemble yourself, being mindful that we draw strength from one another. We must be twined together. Again, when two or more are joined together in the name of the Lord, he is also in the midst. The people who are caught in the world must be reminded of the value of leaning on the Lord.

There should be a distinction to those that know the Lord; it should be evident in our daily walk, and for those who don't know, they should want to know because of the solace or comfort that is exemplified by us. We should not be a deterrent to others.

The tragedy of today is there is no clear distinction between churchgoers and those who don't attend. It would seem as if the church has been influenced by the world rather than the world being influenced by the church. Being set apart means just that, being above the influences of the world and not succumbing to your low desires. Knowing the value of leaning on the Lord and not your own understanding.

Leaning on the Lord and trusting in him to guide our path serves as a barometer or reminder of being steadfast in our convictions and reliance on him to see us through. It may seem passive in the carnal or human consciousness to submit to a force that we can't see. Again, this is in stark contrast between the limitations of the human realm contrasted with the unlimited potential of the fruits of the spirit. As the Bible states, "God is spirit and we must worship him in spirit and truth." We must rise above the human eclipsiation of life.

The challenge that we face in our daily walk is that we want to fight this enormous battle against forces whose express intent is to destroy and devour the human family. When it states that we are transformed by the renewal of our mind, this is not a one-shot deal. This quest is ongoing. When Paul states that daily I die to sin, we are talking about the relentless pursuit of excellence. When they say that the race is not won by the strongest or the swiftest but by the one that endures to the end, it is speaking of those of us who genuinely struggle to live lives aligned with God.

WE MUST REMAIN STEADFAST IN OUR CONVICTIONS and not allow ourselves to succumb to our low desires.

As believers and those who allow themselves to be soldiers in the army of the Lord, we must have full allegiance to the Lord, and we declare victory over an adversarial relationship with God. We don't and will not allow ourselves to submit to a line of reason that is contrary to God's will.

We are not reluctant warriors, but we make a conscious effort to put on the whole armor of God and not allow ourselves to have thoughts or conduct that is contrary to what is expected of us. If a thought comes to us that is contrary to God's province over us, we will not let it take root in our being.

As it is often stated, the battle is in our mind and way of thinking and the thoughts that we hold on to and take root in our consciousness. Again, thoughts become things. As a man thinks, so is he. We must continue to elevate ourselves and consecrate our mind to put a hedge around our crown. The more Christ-centered we become, the more likely it becomes for us to rise above the limitations of the carnal mind. Elevate your mind, and Christ will set you free.

Be Not Conformed to the World

We must lean on the Lord and not our own understanding. In the scheme of things, I evolved to this level of thinking, but as much as I know now, I am still a babe in Christ. I have learned a lot about the Christ consciousness. I have come out of the darkness into the marvelous light. Not knowing of the Christ within me did not afford me the option of knowing who I really was. I was led astray by my own devices, and as the Bible states, man's knowledge pales in comparison to God's.

I have been instructed to rise above the human eclipsiation of life and lean more on the Divine Mind of Christ. Although we are limited in the human realm, we have unlimited potential in the Divine Mind of Christ. The challenge that I face, like Paul stated, is to daily die to the flesh. I began to lean more on the Lord and not my own understanding.

For a person who has been accustomed to leaning on their own understanding, this requires more work than what I tend to do. As it is stated, faith without works is dead. We can talk about it, but we must demonstrate it. As Jesus states, I must be about doing my father's business.

We can become a new creature in Christ if we only believe and accept it as our reality. I must live the life, so God can use me every day in every way. As the Bible states, be not conformed to the world but be transformed by the renewal of your mind. It takes a leap of faith or as it is written don't just be a hearer of the word be a doer of the word.

Accepting my divinity and becoming a new creature in Christ is my quest for living a Christ-centered life. Unlike the computer, which is patterned after the human brain, it is not a simple matter of replacing one chip for another, changing the subsequent behavior. As it is written, one is transformed by the renewal of one's mind. Again, as a man think in his heart so is he. One must embrace a new consciousness or become a new creature in Christ. We must shun the very essence of anything that is contrary to the will of God. As the Bible states, lean on the Lord and not your own understanding, and trust in him with all your might, and he will direct your path.

Any thoughts that come into our mind that are contrary to the will of God are not to be entertained. The process can be likened to a letter that comes to your house that is not yours; you are encouraged to return it to the sender. We should send those thoughts back into the universe because they do not belong to us.

We know that this is a process of reconciliation and allowing ourselves to become reacquainted with our true nature and to awaken that sleeping giant that resides within us and let that Good Spirit have its way with us. The spirit of the Lord is in us yearning to express itself through us and for us. God knows the enormous potential that we have inside of us; he wants us to become reacquainted with it and remember who we really are. In the process of living a life in conforming to the world, we have allowed ourselves to live a life contrary to the will of God and have been accustomed to leaning on our own understanding separate from the will of God.

Consequently, we nurtured and brought forth a consciousness that allowed it to be convenient to live a life consistent with a reprobate mind; therefore, we justify our existence as self-serving, surviving off our lower level needs.

Transformation

"You are transformed by the renewal of your mind."

How many times have we heard this scripture, and how can we make it applicable to our life? This scripture also states be not conformed to this world and also let this mind be in you that is in Christ Jesus.

We must be mindful of the fact that we are made in God's image and likeness. Also, being a form of God, we are equal in part to him. As such, we have the attributes of God inside of us. We are God's manifestation and expression here on earth. God formed us from the dust of the ground and breathed into the nostrils of man and made him a living soul.

We are the manifestation of God; as such, we have the very attributes of God. Therefore, we should exhibit the consciousness of God in all of our endeavors. As Jesus stated, the Father and I are one. We should act and operate in accordance to his will and his desire.

In the scheme of things, we should not be separate from God. We all have the Christ potential inside of us. Christ is the mind of God individualized. We are God's manifestation and expression here on earth. The challenge that we have is to make a conscious effort to let the process work. To lean on the Lord and not our own understanding.

Our goal is to trust in the transformative powers of the mind of Christ, which is the knowledge and wisdom of God unto Salvation. Lift your mind, and Christ will set you free. To be liberated from the constraining thoughts that we impose on ourselves.

We must rise above human obstructions of life and allow the Christ potential to manifest itself. We must allow the process to work to elevate our mind and acknowledge that we have a force inside of us that is greater than anything in the world.

When we come into the realization of what it means to be a Child of God and accept our divinity, as Jesus said, the Father and I are one. To personalize our relationship with God, we must understand that Jesus intended for us to understand the Christ potential that resides in all of mankind. So again, let this mind be in you that was also in Christ Jesus.

Again, we are transformed by the renewal of our mind. It is incumbent upon us that we lean on the Lord and not our own understanding. To let the process work, if there are thoughts that we are holding on to that are contrary to your Christ nature, don't let them take root in your mind. The similitude is likened to a letter that comes to your house; you should promptly return it to the sender.

Don't hold on to thoughts that are detrimental to your Spiritual Wellness. Don't let them take root in your mind. It is incumbent upon us as believers to furnish the life and live in direct accordance to the commandments of God.

The ancient Sanskrit word for "man" is "think." We must remember that Christ is the mind of God individualized. We all have the Christ potential inside of us. Christ is a personification; it's not confined to a person, region, or time. It is a universal consciousness that we all are privy to.

With that in mind, we must allow the process to work and remain steadfast in our convictions. To ask and expect God to deliver on his promise. As David said, "I once was young but now I am old, I have never seen the righteous forsaken or seed go begging for bread."

The thoughts that we hold unto have a self-fulfilling prophesy. Thoughts are things and words materialized. As a man thinks in his heart so is he. We must be mindful of the thoughts we harbor in our mind because they become our reality. Lest we forget we are spirits housed in a body. We must rise above our human eclipsiation where the natural order is to promote our humanness over divinity.

Contrary to that notion, become aware of the awesome power waiting to be used. Everything that has and will be created exist on the idealized level. Our way of thinking is so critical in obtaining what we desire and need from God. We must begin to live a life consistent with the will of God and not have a will that is contrary to his.

We Are Transformed by the Renewal of Our Mind

It is often stated that as a man thinks in his heart so is he. Essentially, thoughts become things. With that in mind, I am a thinker. Like so many people, I think about my past, I think about my present, and I think about my future.

Sometimes, I feel I put too much thought into things and not enough action. It is good to think about things, but it comes a time to put things into action. As the Bible states, faith without works is dead. It is good to have ideas, but unless you put them into action, they are just a dream.

Right now, I feel that I am living below my expectations, and I am consumed with doubt and need reassurance like what I want to do is not achievable because of the limitations that I impose upon myself.

Yet in contrast, I spend so much of my time and energy encouraging others and reassuring them of their abilities, yet I go lacking. As the Bible states, if no one is encouraging you, then you must encourage yourself. I must ask myself am I that consumed with doubt that

I lack faith in my intrinsic ability to overcome the obstacles that I have imposed upon myself.

Have I become a person with so little faith in myself that I am unwilling to try to change the direction of my life, yet I aspire to motivate others to achieve the things that they desire? I have to ask myself where this doubt comes from. Surely if others can see my potential, then I should be able to see it, too.

People are inspired by my words and the insight that I express. Since it comes from me, then it must be of me.

When I expound on this consciousness that exceeds our wildest imagination, I exclude myself from the process by not incorporating it into my way of life. I ask myself am I not worthy of this process as well.

The thoughts that I desire for others is something that I desire for myself as well. It is imperative to me that I should self-actualize as well. I must become a new creature in Christ and Christ is the mind of God individualized.

To become a new creature in Christ, I must acknowledge my oneness with God. As Jesus said, the Father and I are one. To be on one accord with God despite the circumstances. To lean on the Lord and not my own understanding. To let this mind be in me that was also in Christ Jesus.

The challenge that we face is to rise above the human eclipsiation of life and not let our divine qualities be overshadowed by our human qualities. Be mindful that we are made in the image and likeness of God, and as such, we are a form of God.

God did not create us for sport or play. No, to the contrary, he created us in the best of molds for his express intentions. He needed a body to house his Spirit, so he made man. We are Spirits housed in a body first and foremost.

As the Bible states, be not conformed to this world but be transformed by the renewal of your mind. The thing that made Jesus so distinguishable is that he recognized his divinity and lived accordingly and so should we.

As it is written, great things have I done, but greater things shall you do.

The question that I put forth to myself and to others: *am I willing to do the work to let the process work to furnish the life so that God can use me to live a Christ-centered life?*

Living My Life Like It's Golden

To live a Christ-centered life would require that we would live in accordance to the will of God irrespective to what is going on. As they said of Job to display SPIRITUAL INTEGRITY to hold on to God's unchanging hands and know whatever problem we have that God can work it out. To walk by faith and not by sight. To accept the fact that God doesn't put any more on us than what we can bear.

To furnish the life so that God can use us. We must remain steadfast in our convictions and lean on the Lord and not our own understanding. To petition the Lord and let him know what our needs are.

We must have the faith to know that whatever we need God has it, and that we can do all things through Christ that strengthens us.

We are limited in the human realm, but we have unlimited potential in the divine mind of Christ as Eric Butterworth states. When we come into the realization of what it means to be Christ like, there will be no limit to what we can achieve. Christ is the mind of God individualized. As it is written, let this mind be in you that was also in Christ Jesus who being a form of God did not consider it robbery to be equal to God.

God made man in his image and likeness. He formed man from the dust of the ground, breathed into his nostrils, and made him a living soul. When we come into the realization of who we are and rise above our self-imposed limitations and accept the divine attributes of our nature, we will realize how proud we are.

Being confident about our divinity and not being fearful or doubtful of it. As Jesus stated, the Father and I are one. To know that God created us for a specific purpose with noble intentions. That he gave mankind DOMINION OVER HIS CREATION is a testament to what we are endowed with.

We are God's manifestation and expression here on earth. God needed a place to house his spirit, so he made man. Essentially, we are made in God's image and likeness; therefore, the natural order is for us to be on one accord with God irrespective to the appearance of things. We should stay close to the source and not allow anything to separate us from our creator.

What Is Going On in 2010?

For a people who have survived in the wilderness of North America as Elijah Muhammad has described our odyssey in America, we have been out of slavery for over one hundred years, and we have recently received our civil rights or equal protection in the past fifty years. We are a story. In contrast it is the best of times and yet as some would describe it, or the worst of times for Black America.

The stark contrast is evident in the fact that America elected its first Black president by a decisive margin. Yet the schism in Black America is so clear it would appear as if we have an adversarial relationship within the Black community. At one point, we displayed a more uniformed position on most things.

We would embrace one another instead of recoiling from one another. We would be God-fearing people who took their relationship with God personal, and it showed. We looked to God for direction and guidance and trusted in the process.

In our recent past, our focus was on self-reliance and having control over the institutions that affected us. We wanted a greater representation and a presence of people who looked like us in positions of leadership. Also, we wanted a voice in the issues that affected us and our community.

Well fast forward to 2010, and you'll see we have people who look like us in the decision-making process. Regarding issues of self-reliance, we have abandoned that for a posture of apathy and self-centeredness. Also, the notion of self-sufficiency has been thrown out the window with the bath water; sadly, most of the institutions in our community are owned by people that largely reside outside of our community. Monies that are generated from within our community are routinely leaving our community, siphoning off the wealth of our community and making others filthy rich.

Institutions that, back in the day, were fertile ground for fueling the vitality of our community are now diminishing seemingly in importance.

The family, the nucleus of existence, would seem to be under siege. As high as 70 percent of the homes in our community do not have a father in them, which throws the pendulum of stability off the mark because who is there to protect the village?

Added to that is an apathetic concern for education by today's youth as well as a curriculum that again has the appearance of not addressing the needs of this cohort of children whose energy and passion is being consumed by a counterculture that says it isn't cool to get an education. Compounding the fact is a proliferation of religious institutions that are steeped in traditions and costumes that are not serving the needs of the people, resulting in a populace that is disengaged from the church.

What is even more alarming is the absence of vibrancy. We have a community that is stifled and disconnected from seeing its intrinsic brilliance because of its benign neglect and virtual omission of a sensitivity and responsiveness to its own needs. With that in mind, there is a critical need to revisit not our distant past but recent events when people were so passionate and concerned about doing something to change their position themselves.

We don't have to reinvent the wheel; the most important thing is for us to revisit the same things that made a difference, for us to rely on one another and to get to know who we are and whose we are. God never intended for us to be disconnected from one another. It was his express intent and desire for us to have dominion over this earth and to be his manifestation and expression here on earth. Genesis 1:26 states that we are made in God's image and likeness, and as such, we are a form of God.

Our disconnectedness from God causes us to act and conduct our affairs in a manner that is directly contrary to God's will and design.

We don't surrender to God, no, we surrender to a life force that is contrary to our nature. As the Bible states, we should be in the world but not of the world. We recognize that we are in the world but again the Bible expressly states that we should not be conformed to the world, but we should be transformed by the renewal of our mind. It goes on to state let this mind be in you that is also in Christ Jesus.

As we all know, the thoughts that we harbor become a self-fulfilling prophesy; our thoughts become things. We have been taught that thoughts are things and words materialized. As a man thinks so is he. The thought process has been likened to receiving letters that come to your home as the similitude goes: "if a letter comes to your home that is not yours you are encouraged to promptly return that letter to the sender." Such is the case of holding on to thoughts that are contrary to the will of God; we should not be consumed with any thoughts that cause us to be in a state that is contrary to the nature of God.

We have been instructed to live a righteous life, one that God is pleased with because God cannot live in an unclean vessel. Being in a state of consciousness that causes us to operate in a manner that causes dis-ease is fertile ground for dissonance or disconnectedness from our source. The similitude is that of purchasing a new automobile and throwing the manual away not adhering to the specifications of the designers or noncompliance to the maintenance of any sorts. Consequently, you expedite the decay and subsequent destruction of what was once a fine automobile.

Again, we must be mindful that God is our inexhaustible vein of supply and that whatever we need God has it. It is imperative to us and for us to lean on the Lord and not our own understanding. To trust in him with all our might and to not let anything separate us from God. As the Bible states, the expression on our face is the index of our heart.

When we say this little light of ours were going to let it shine wherever we go, it should be evident not by what we say but by what we do. We must honor the fact that we are God's manifestation and expression here on earth and that God made this earth and he entrusted it to us.

Remember that God created us in his image and likeness and formed us from the dust of the ground. From a scientific perspective, there is no distinction from the composition of the dirt on this planet and the proportion of water that is on this planet and the corresponding composition of humans; our body and the earth are one. The earth is our domicile, our place to reside, but we come from God who "formed man from the dust of the ground, breathed into his nostrils and made him a living soul."

Again, we are a form of God, and as such, we are God's manifestation and expression here on earth. With that in mind, God created this earth for his purpose and intent to glorify him.

When he created it, he gave man dominion over everything, and dominion means supreme authority. WE HAVE TO HONOR THE COMMANDMENTS OF ALMIGHTY GOD, to live a life that is consistent with his nature and submit to his will relentlessly. As the Bible states, "GOD IS SPIRIT AND WE SHOULD WORSHIP HIM IN SPIRIT AND TRUTH." We should live and act as if we are in the very presence of God.

Reconciliation

God breathed into the nostrils of man and made him a living soul. The word breath and the word spirit come from the same root word. Essentially, the spirit of the Lord is within us. Consequently, there is no need to go outside of ourselves to get God's attention. We spend an inordinate amount of time ingesting substances or spirits to get relief in our ignorance of things. Yet the spirit that we have by nature we neglect to harness the power within ourselves. As Jesus stated, greater is that which is in you than that which is in the world. Jesus also said great things have I done but greater things shall you do. Let this mind be in you that is also in Christ Jesus.

We often talk about Jesus and glorify his presence in our life, yet we have not come to the greater realization that the same force that resides within him also resides within us all.

The Spirit resides within us all. The unique thing about Jesus is that he realized his divinity and mastered it. As it has been stated, we have customarily associated the semantic connection of Christ and Jesus as one. When the two are separate and distinct entities.

Christ is the knowledge and wisdom of God unto salvation. Essentially, it is a consciousness and not a person. Christ is the mind of God individualized. As Jesus stated, the Father and I are one. We have been told to rise above the human eclipsiation of life to allow our divine or spiritual nature to govern our behavior. Not to be ruled by our lower desires and to succumb to anything that is contrary to God's will. To lean on the Lord and not our own understanding. To allow our Godly persona to manifest itself wholeheartedly.

We must acknowledge that God is our inexhaustible vein of supply and that whatever we need God has it. We must be mindful of the fact that there is no failure with God. In the carnal or shall we say the design of this system is to live a life separate and distinct from God.

We tend to rely on a consciousness that excludes God. In the human realm, it becomes easy to attribute our accomplishments and gains to our own devices, our education, our degrees, our intelligence or anything other than God.

As a culture, we have allowed ourselves and convinced ourselves that it is okay to glorify the creation and not the creator. We have allowed ourselves to become disconnected from our spirituality and to embrace a consciousness that really is foreign to us. We have justified our separation as a natural concomitant of contemporary living. Everyone else is doing it why should we be different. But this is where our journey is different.

We are supposed to be set apart. We are to be in the world but not of the world.

We are to glorify God always and to be one with him irrespective to what is going on. Our God is a jealous God, and we should not put anything before him or live a life that is contrary to his will. THE BIBLE STATES THAT WE SUFFER NEEDLESSLY AND

THAT WE SHOULD KEEP GOD'S COMMANDMENTS AND LIVE.

Holding on to God's unchanging hands and remaining steadfast in our convictions has been the cornerstone of our existence. To be delivered from external oppression only to be oppressed by ourselves, we have allowed ourselves to be held captive by a mindset that is diametrically opposed to the will of God. Perpetuating a destructive mentality of passivity and being consumed with the distinct notion of something or someone else saving us other than ourselves.

Before we can have authority over anything, we must have authority over ourselves. We must let this mind be in us that is also in Christ Jesus. Not to be conformed to this world but to be transformed by the renewal of our mind. We must let the process work. The thoughts that we harbor are so important to us and for us.

Submitting to God's will without hesitation, to lean on the Lord and not our own understanding. To trust in that Good Spirit to guide and direct our path. To not allow ourselves to be entangled in the toils and tribulations of this life. To rise above the human obstructions and let the Christ consciousness rule and super rule us. To lean on the Lord and not our own understanding. To recognize and realize that Christ is the knowledge and wisdom of God unto salvation. Accepting the fact that there is no failure with God and that if God can't do it can't be done.

As a people, we must come into a better and fuller understanding of what it means to be a child of God, that we are made in the image and likeness of God, and as such, we are a form of God. We have the very attributes of God within us. Essentially, it is only natural that we should be one with God. As Jesus stated, the Father and I are one. Christ when viewed as a consciousness states that Christ is the mind of God individualized. Consequently, it is unnatural for us to allow ourselves to be separate from God. As it is stated, we should love what God loves and hate what he hates.

When we come to accept our divinity as Jesus accepted his, it allows us to rise above the limitations of the human consciousness and extend ourselves to the unlimited potential of the Christ. As Jesus stated, great things have I done but greater things shall you do. Being mindful that Christ is the mind of God individualized. People as they reflect on their current circumstances are quick to state that this is as good as it gets. To the contrary, despite the appearance of things, the best is yet to come. It is God's good pleasure that we should live an abundant life. That we should come to know ourselves as God knows us.

That we should live a spirit-filled life and realize first and foremost that we are spirits housed in a body.

Reconciliation requires that we reconnect with the source that we come from and let the Spirit of the Lord manifest itself within us and through us. To put more trust in God and to lean on him and not our own understanding to know that he is our inexhaustible vein of supply. God did not create us for sport or play. He gave us authority over everything that exists. For that authority to manifest itself, we must allow ourselves to be one with God and to recognize that we are God's manifestation and expression here on earth.

Letting Go and Letting God

As simplistic as it may sound, when we surrender to God and let him have his way with us, we tend to do better. Letting the process work is the key to our salvation and being led by the Spirit and not by the ego or our own design. We must remain steadfast in our convictions and turn to God often in our affairs. First and foremost, we must pray and ask God for guidance and humble ourselves to a critical need that we have as believers, to petition God.

Since we come from God, it is only natural to refer to him for directions. Essentially, he is our owner's manual. Just as the similitude of a car having an owner's manual with specifications to follow. Also, that car has maintenance schedule and preferred manner to sustain it. Petitioning God is essential for maintaining a relationship and connection with the prescribed way to conduct our affairs and the direction to take. Complying is critical to us maintaining the proper relationship with God and one another.

Essentially, complying in the eyesight of God is keeping his commandments, therefore keeping the consciousness that he has decreed for us. The natural order for us is to be one with God and to live a life that is in accordance with his commandments. As one would say, to live a life as if we were in the very presence of God. Consider that God is omnipresent in every vacant place. The natural order would be to conduct our behaviors and affairs as if we are in his presence. Consistent with the concept that we are held accountable for our words, thoughts, and deeds. With that in mind, God does expect a lot out of us. But be mindful that God knows what we are fully capable of, for aren't we made in his image and likeness?

We are made in God's image and likeness, and as such, we are a form of God, having the very attributes of God. We are God's expression and manifestation here on earth. As it is stated, we are spirits housed in a body. God gave mankind dominion over his creation, and dominion means supreme authority. Before we can have authority over anything, we must exercise authority over ourselves. It is imperative that we govern as God would govern in a manner that reflects his majesty in a wise and prudent manner. Mankind is a valuable entity in the eyesight of God, and he expects a lot of creation, for he created us in the best of molds.

We must let go of anything that is contrary to the will of God and rise above the human impediments to lift up our mind and let Christ set us free. Christ is the knowledge and wisdom of Almighty God unto salvation. We need to lean on the Lord and not our own understanding, to trust in the Lord to guide and direct our path. As Jesus would say, the Father and I are one. To come into a greater awareness of what it means when it is said that the Father and I are one. Christ has been described as the mind of God individualized. In contemporary terms, when one begins to acknowledge his divinity or oneness with God, it would have the appearance of being blasphemous.

Contrary to that notion, we must become more acquainted with our true nature. We are more than flesh and blood. That we are God's manifestation and expression here on earth and that God formed us in his image and likeness and breathed into the nostrils of man and made him a living soul. That God gave us dominion over all his creation, and dominion means supreme authority.

God would not have given us the assignment if he didn't know we could accomplish it. For whom God calls he does qualify them for the assignment.

It is imperative that we begin to act and conduct ourselves in a manner that is consistent with our spiritual nature. To lean on the Lord and not our own understanding. To trust in him with all our might. To live a spirit-filled life.

GOD IS SPIRIT, SO WE MUST WORSHIP HIM IN SPIRIT AND TRUTH, AND RISE ABOVE THE HUMAN ECLIPSIATON OF LIFE.

Spiritual Integrity

People often state tough times don't last but tough people do. With that in mind, think about Job. A man who was a faithful servant. God chooses him as a man who exemplified spiritual integrity. A man who even in the face of adversity remained steadfast in his conviction. Despite prevailing conditions that seemed insurmountable, he held on to God's unchanging hands even when his friends and wife tried to convince him to curse God and die. He viewed them all as foolish individuals with so little faith, who like a lot of people hold on to God when things are going well but become doubtful when difficulties are presented to them.

Doubting ourselves is one thing but doubting the God that is in us is another. Learning how to lean on the Lord in the time of troubles and difficulties is something that requires a lot of humility as opposed to being humiliated by our circumstances. Oftentimes in our ego driven society or consciousness, we find ourselves facing our difficulties in a manner that excludes God.

We tend to lean on ourselves and not the Lord. But the Bible states to trust in the Lord with all your might. It also goes on to state that we suffer needlessly.

One apparent advantage of leaning on the Lord is that we are in full compliance with his commandments. We're connected to an inexhaustible vein of supply which affords us an opportunity to live an abundant life, one that he is pleased with. Again, being made in his image and likeness, we are to conduct ourselves as if we are in the very presence of God. Essentially to maintain standards of conduct consistent with his majesty.

Despite prevailing conditions, we are to hold onto God's unchanging hands.

God wants us to have a spiritual awakening, to come into the fullness of what it means to be a child of God and to act accordingly. To get more out of God, we must be busy doing his work. We must focus on elevation and live a life according to the dictates of almighty God as we have been exhorted to live right or furnish the life so God can use us. We must allow the mind of God to manifest itself in us. The good thing for us is it's already there waiting to be utilized.

Spiritual Integration

To live in accordance to the commandments of God—that should be our quest. As the Bible states, keep God's commandments and live. God is Spirit, so we must worship him in Spirit and Truth.

Spiritual matters are spiritually discerned. We must live a life consistent and compatible with the source that we come from. We are in the world but not of the world. We were given the directive not to be conformed to this world but be transformed by the renewal of our mind.

The process can be likened to the process of complying to the manufacturer's specifications of an automobile. The automobile comes with a manual and specifications to be followed to produce the best results.

The manufacturer gives detailed analysis of how to best maintain the car to yield the best results as well. All this was done to facilitate the best relationship between the owner and his car with the understanding that one would be in full compliance to get the best results.

Such is the case with mankind. God made man in his image and likeness. He formed man from the dust of the ground and breathed into the nostrils of man and made him a living soul.

Now with that in mind, being that we are a form of God, we are expected to operate in a manner that is consistent with the manner of God. We are instructed to be on one accord with God always and to live a Christ-centered life to acknowledge God in all our endeavors. To lean on the Lord always. As Jesus stated, the Father and I are one.

To trust in God with all our might. To know and appreciate the Godly presence that resides in you. To accept your divinity and rise above the human eclipsiation of life and lean more on the divine mind of Christ.

Jesus recognized his divinity and so should we. As he stated, he and the Father were one. Christ is the knowledge and wisdom of God unto salvation. Christ is the mind of God individualized.

Think About What You Think About

Just because you are in a transition doesn't mean you have to be in a freefall. Here I am, Lord, use me in your service, draw me nearer to thee as it is written we cannot serve God from afar. As Jesus stated, we must be on one accord with God irrespective to what is going on. It is our separation from God that is the root of our problems.

I am learning the value of trusting in the Lord because right now he has my undivided attention. As the songs goes, through many dangers, toils, and snares, I have already come. It was grace that brought me through it all. If it wasn't for the Lord on my side, where would I be? With all the challenges that I have experienced, I never would have made it if it had not been for the Lord watching over me.

As they say faith is the substance of things hoped for and the evidence of things unseen. We must believe that God will see us through. I can do all things through the God in me that sustains me despite me being me. God truly is a watchman on the wall. He has brought me out of the darkness into the marvelous light. For that, I am truly grateful.

I know what I know now in large part because of my experiences and sometimes those experiences were not so pleasant. As my dad would say, I may not be the man that I want to be, but I thank God I am not the man that I was. Again, just because I am going through something doesn't mean I have to be in a freefall.

Right now, not only am I away from my residency, but my entire family is residing in different locales.

Our utilities have been turned off once again for the fourth time within a year. We still have unresolved property tax issues. In conjunction with that, my hours have been cut at my job.

But all is not lost. This is time to be like Job and display and convey spiritual integrity to hold on to God's unchanging hands knowing that he has a way out for the faithful. Embracing the notion that despite things, all of God's days are good. That I willingly embrace him unwaveringly knowing that he will not forsake me or leave me alone.

I know that he did not bring me this far to leave me alone. It is up to me to follow his commandments and live a spirit-filled existence and let him do his perfect work through me. God knows that we get worn and weary, but the race is not won by the strongest or the swiftest but the one that endures to the end. Our crisis should be viewed as opportunities for God to demonstrate his might.

I must rise above the constraints that I have imposed upon myself and lean on the divine mind of Christ. Christ is the knowledge and wisdom of God unto salvation. Although we are limited in the human realm of our existence, we have unlimited potential in the divine mind of Christ. It is imperative that I and the God in me that I can do nothing except what is revealed to me by God. To God be the glory.

We Are Transformed by the Renewal of Our Mind

I may not be the man that I aspire to be, but I thank God that I am not the man that I was. Free your mind, and the rest will follow. When you change the way you think, your situation will change. We are creatures of habit and what our thought patterns are.

As the Bible states, as a man thinks in his heart so is he. Our thoughts become self-fulfilling prophesy. Thoughts are things and words materialized. With that in mind, it is time to revisit my way of thinking and learn how to appreciate myself.

I spend the greater part of my day encouraging and motivating others. Now it is time to take my own advice and live the life that I aspire to achieve. I read and talk about it, and now it is time to live the life that I talk and write about. This is my time.

A New Creature in Christ

I understand the theory and the philosophy, but now is the time to start demonstrating it. Let this mind be in me that was also in Christ Jesus who being a form of God did not consider it robbery to be equal to God.

Lean on the Lord and not your own understanding, and trust in him with all your might, and he will direct your path. Man's knowledge pales in comparison to God's. We suffer needlessly. We must agree with God and form an alliance with him. Hold on to God's unchanging hands with the full understanding that whatever we need God has it. For God is our inexhaustible vein of supply; we cannot allow ourselves to be separated from God.

I will henceforth accept that it's expected and possible for me to live a Christ-centered existence and that I cannot accept anything else. That I will focus on elevation and make a concerted effort to be on one accord with God always.

It is the God in me that will be the driving force. No longer will I look for others to validate me, but I shall know with a surety that whatever I need God has it.

I will accept a prayerful posture throughout the day, and I will consecrate my thoughts and not entertain thoughts that are contrary to the will of God.

I will remain steadfast in my convictions and will not allow myself to be consumed with doubt or fear.

I will have a timeframe for any adversarial relationships whether that be with myself or others. Settle your disputes with your adversaries quickly.

I will acknowledge God in all my endeavors and consult him in all my affairs and live in accordance to his will always irrespective to circumstances.

Perseverance

I am still in the race, and the beauty of it all is that I still have a chance if I hold on to God's unchanging hands and know that he will guide and direct my path.

I will acknowledge God in all my ways and lean on him and not my own understanding, for he is my inexhaustible vein of supply. He has brought me from a mighty long way, for he brought me out of the darkness into the marvelous light, and for that, I am truly grateful.

I must cultivate a better relationship with my Godly persona and appreciate myself as a child of God. Heretofore, I have been accustomed to thinking of ego driven or humanness contrasted with my spirituality.

In the human realm of existence, I am limited, but in the divine mind of Christ, I have unlimited potential. Just as it was stated by Jesus, great things have I done, but greater things shall you do. We must recognize the Christ potential in us.

Christ is the knowledge and wisdom of God unto salvation. To be Christ like is to be God like. As Jesus stated, the Father and I are one. I am saying all this right now, but there is another Spirit that I must interject right now and that is the Spirit of my mother.

When I think about a mother's presence, I am mindful of the unconditional love that God extends to us; that is what is missing in my life. My love of the Lord is so strong and pronounced because it gives me surety in the absence of my mother.

Now I have had some phenomenal mother figures who have assisted me on my journey and made my way much easier. I am sure that the women I have loved shared traits of my mother in their own respective way, for they all filled a void in my life.

It is times like this when I must acknowledge or clarify my feelings, something that I tend to avoid doing. I am mindful and acknowledge my father often.

But for the most part, there isn't much verbalization of my mother's presence. Her presence is mostly on an unconscious manner, for hers is evident in the consciousness that I exude.

The gentle, nurturing, compassionate nature that is evident in my job as a caregiver but also extended to those that I extend care to in my daily walk—she impacted upon me and left her mark on me in so many ways. She took up so much time with me and gave me so much attention as if she was preparing me for this journey.

She understood me and let me be me. On reflection, as I write and think about it, I can feel her presence and watchful eye, the guidance and reassurance she embedded in me. She knew just what to say and do to get the best results from me.

It has been a blessing to work in a setting where there have been so many women around me. I get high praises because of the way I treat women and how I conduct myself.

Please forgive me, I must acknowledge the role that my daughters have played in my life as well, for they have added surety as well as security to my existence.

In my formative years as a young father, a thought that was revealed to me was how can I treat another man's daughter wrong and be okay with that, but expect someone to treat my daughters right? I was always conscientious of how I treated women.

Being influenced by the love that I had for my mother and my daughters, I always wanted to be viewed in a positive light because I didn't want to be viewed in a hypocritical manner. I did not want to tell them it is the nature of man to conduct themselves in an unruly manner or conceded fashion. In contrast a real man operates in a manner that is pleasing to God to bring forth his finer qualities.

Being mindful that we learn something from everyone, we even learn from the mistakes of others or from our own mistakes if we are fortunate and God finds favor with us. There were things that I did not always understand, but because of God's grace and mercy that he extended to me, I have been afforded an opportunity to grow to a level beyond my most vivid imagination

My mother envisioned this day in which I would be given a chance to come to know the presence of God within myself. I watched my mother pray for deliverance from what was a long and lengthy grief-stricken odyssey. The year was 1970, and it started with a bang and ended with a boom. But through all the trials and tribulations, the turbulence, the grief, the agony, we held on to God's unchanging hands.

Had it not been for the prayers of the righteous and our unwavering belief in almighty God and his transformative powers, we never would have made it. Our family was shaken at the foundations of everything that we believed in.

In 1970, I began adulthood and became a man, a role that I was capitulated into that God had already assigned me to unbeknownst to me at the time. But on reflection, my parents had always kept close watch over me. Their objective was to keep me on the straight and narrow path, to operate in a manner that was pleasing to God irrespective to the appearance of circumstances.

As a child, I always felt that my parents were overprotective of me, but it took being a parent to understand the process and the corresponding benefits to be reaped. Had it not been for them keeping their loving arms of protection around me, I would not understand that is what God does for us all.

God truly is a watchman on the wall, and he keeps his loving arms of protection around us. We must follow God's commandments and live a spirit-filled existence. As it is written, we must lean on the Lord and not our own understanding, and trust in him with all our might, and he will direct our path.

Through it all, being compliant with my parents' wishes kept me from being devoured from adversities surrounding me and an adversarial relationship that had developed within myself. A decade of distress best describes our family dynamics. My father experienced a health challenge that would alter his life. A brother got involved in a major altercation with the police that changed the pattern of his life as well. Another brother whose life was being impacted upon by an emerging drug epidemic not only altered the nature of our community and country but his life as well.

All these variables going on within our home at a time when I was developing a penchant for marijuana and girls not necessarily in that order.

I had planned that summer to explore them both, but God had other plans for me and that was the beginning of an altered existence for me as well. This was the beginning of what would become my Spiritual Awakening.

When I reflect on this era, I can the see the importance of having a submissive nature and a willing to be obedient to the guidance of your parents. I was always cognizant of the impact that my actions had on my parents. There is a discourse from the Bible that focuses on the importance of your faith amid troubles. It comes from Romans 5:3-4: Not only this; but we also rejoice in sufferings, knowing that sufferance produces endurances; and endurance character; and character hope.

In group discussion with a client, I referred to the often-quoted statement when one gets to the end of their rope, one should tie a knot in it and hold on. His response added another dimension to the often-repeated statement; he stated that one should tie a knot in it and pull themselves up. Be ever so mindful that this is not as good as it gets. The best is yet to come if you only believe.

Dear Joshua

It's our time to go to another level. We need to be on a better accord. Something went wrong somewhere, and now is the time to go forward with a fresh start. We blame one another, and the truth of the matter is we both are responsible for the direction that we take now. For it is the here and now that matters the most.

We both can be a hot mess, but we both deserve better. What's interesting is that my father and I had a period where we were distant from one another. I regretted that because we both needed one another. The issue for us is that we are more of a father and son disconnection as opposed to a distant stepfather. That seems to be the case, but in all actuality, you are my son.

I am the one that has been in your life throughout the span of your recognition and awareness. I have been a part of your life for as long as you have known yourself. Your earliest recognition of things in you or around you, I was there. The first drum set, I was there. Your earliest memories of the Dominion, I was there as well. I am etched in your memories.

When we walked in the neighborhood on St. Aubin, those are fond memories that can't be erased. Yes, there were mistakes that were made. But that doesn't mean that I didn't love you, and I didn't care. There is no book on parenting that covers everything. Because it really is an experience that requires your willingness to learn. Essentially you become a better parent the more involved you are in the process.

I watch how engaging you are with my nephew, and I can see how much you have grown. One thing we must be mindful of is that we grow into our greatness. Nowhere is that more evident in being a parent. No one comes here readymade. We do make mistakes, that is a fact, but with diligence and determination we can overcome ourselves.

I reflect when Paris was making her arrival and how overwhelmed you were. You had the look of bewilderment; like what am I going to do? I recognize the look because I had the same look in my eyes and how I so wanted my father to give me reassurance that I would be all right. That was a challenge for me, getting reassurance from someone else. That's just where I was; I thought so much of my father, and I was disappointed in his response. That was the root of our disconnection. At a critical time in my life, when I needed him, he wasn't there for me.

The fact that we were separate from one another, I felt like a ship without a rudder. I needed his guidance, and he wasn't there. So, I say all this to you for a reason. Search yourself to see where our separation began. The events leading up to it and how it made you feel. Because for us to go forward, we must go back. Some things run deep because we must deal with the emotions connected with it as well.

I know we direct a lot of anger towards ourselves but we must get to the root of the problem and be honest with ourselves. Because there's a reason for everything. I know that I must have disappointed you or discouraged you, so let's allow ourselves to be transparent. My father and I got off track, and that division lasted for too long, and that was time we could not get back. Let's learn from one another and bring closure to this aspect of our relationship.

Let's go to the next level. I offer a sincere apology for all the wrong I have done. The hurtful things that I have said. For the tongue truly is the unruliest organ in the body. Words do have a lot of power. For the power of life and death is in the tongue. We can speak things into existence.

So, it's with that in mind we speak and invoke the will of the creator and let him direct our affairs. In the biblical accord, it states: "Lean on the Lord and not your own understanding and trust him with all your might, and he will direct our path." We say that we can do all things through Christ that strengthens us; that should be our mantra.

We can overcome anything that we choose to. For everything exist first and foremost in the thought realm. As Lord Shaffer would always state, focus on elevation. To rise above the human eclipsiation of life and lean more on the divine mind of Christ. We don't fully realize how much potential we really have. As Prophet Jones said, although we act like midgets we are giants.

Our condition can change, but before it changes, our mindset or way of thinking must change. As Lord Shaffer said, we can do it. Saying all that, it is time for us to change how we deal with each other. We do have a choice in the matter. I think about all the time that my father and I lost before we got back on one accord. By the time that he and I got back on a better accord, he was dying.

But, we are taught that if we have life in our body, we still have a chance. I think where I was when my father and I began to communicate with each other. It was thirty years ago. Interestingly enough, like yourself, I had just injured my arm. I fell off a bike and fractured my arm. I was off work for six weeks.

What is peculiar is that prior to the injury, I had stated that if I had six weeks I could get my affairs together. I was just going through a lot of ongoing challenges, and it was just time to make some major adjustments to my life experiences. I wasn't expecting the injury, but when it happens, it put things in perspective.

Out of that decision came other decisions that ultimately led to me meeting you and your mother. Life is full of a lot of twist and turns, and like they say, you know where you been, but you have no idea what is in store for you.

For everything that God has is good and very good. When I met you, everything just lined up in an orderly fashion. I was enjoying my life, but I needed more out of life than what I was getting. Even though I had an apartment, when I moved in, my thoughts were that I would be there for three years. Three years later, we moved to St. Aubin, and the rest is history.

I cannot change the fact that I am not your biological father, but I was of the understanding that we could deal with that. For I was the father that God put in your path because you needed one. I have fallen short in that role, and I can't change the manner and the way that our relationship unfolded. It Is like a line from the movie *He Got Game*: "God forgives so why don't you."

I had to learn how to forgive my father, but I also had to learn how to forgive myself for the role that I played in our estrangement. I can always say how I felt. But did I ever take the time to consider his needs or his concerns? My father had his challenges—some I knew about and some that I never even considered.

But, I did come to the realization that he did the best that he knew how to do with the understanding that he had. That's the advantage of forgiveness is that it provides an opportunity to not just consider your needs but the needs of others. For we can justify our actions and proceed accordingly. What we must be mindful of is that the creator expects more out of us than what he is getting.

He encourages us to extend love to one another even when we don't feel inclined to do so. I know that we have hurt one another; we cannot continue this way. We are lost and wandering in the wilderness. But it's time to cut that spirit off and move forward with a new vision. As well as a renewed mind. For it truly is a mind thing. For thoughts are things, and words do materialize. We can't just be hearers of the word; we must be doers of the word. Essentially, to practice what we preach.

Sincerely,
Dad

Abundant Grace

It is important that we have a sense of clarity in our thoughts and not be lukewarm in our convictions and those things that we aspire to achieve. Not being steadfast or having surety of ourselves causes us to be double-minded. As the Bible states, a double-minded person is unstable in all their ways. God is not the author of confusion. He wants us to be blessed and to have an abundant life. It is imperative that we come to trust in the Lord.

Jesus stated, "Verily, verily, I say unto you. He that believeth on me. The works that I do shall he do also." Jesus recognized and realized that he and the Father were one, and so should we. We cannot undermine our spiritual essence by allowing ourselves to be separate from God. We allow ourselves to be separate from God, and we let ourselves be led astray by our own desires and inhibitions, the thoughts that we harbor that are contrary to God's will. When Peter walked on the water without doubting the process, he was doing fine, but the moment he allowed doubt to creep into his mind, he abruptly began to sink.

When we allow fear and doubt to consume us and take root in our mind, we allow ourselves to be disconnected from the source that created us. Asking God for something and doubting his ability to deliver on his promise causes us to waver in our convictions. Consequently, we are easily uprooted when trials and tribulations come our way. We must remain steadfast in our convictions and like Job, have spiritual integrity. He knew the Lord would take care of him; he didn't have any doubt in his mind.

We are made in God's image and likeness, and as such we have enormous potential to achieve extraordinary things exceeding our most vivid imagination. We know these are perilous times, and it appears God has forsaken us. But to the contrary, this is not as good as it gets. No, the best is yet to come if we only believe. For the Bible states: "Except the time is cut short for the elect's sake we shall all perish." No God in his infinite mercy will not allow us to perish. He has given the faithful a way out; he did not create mankind for sport or play. He created this earth to be a paradise for us to live in peace and harmony.

He created us to be his manifestation and expression here on earth. We are spirits housed in a body; we are God's representation here on earth. God created this earth with the intentions for us to govern it in a manner that was designed to please him in accordance to his commandments. In accordance to his will and no other way it was not designed to be governed in a way that is contrary to his will and for man's distinct pleasure. As the Bible states, keep God's commandment and live.

The key to our existence is to live a Christ-centered life. Being mindful that Christ is a consciousness that Jesus personified and so can we. Christ is the knowledge and wisdom of God unto salvation. It is a universal consciousness that all mankind has privy to use. It is not constrained to a region, a time, an idiom, or ethnicity. We all have the Christ potential within us. The Spirit of the Lord resides within us all. God told us to have peace, be still, and know who he is. We must awaken the I AM consciousness that resides within us all.

The Bible states, "Let this mind be in you that is also in Christ Jesus." The Bible states we suffer needlessly as evidenced by letting ourselves harbor thoughts and live a life that is contrary to his will. When we live a life that is contrary to God's will, it causes us to have an existence that is not pleasing to God and wreaks havoc on us and our fellow man; we undermine ourselves and leave one open to destruction and decadence.

Gratitude

As Princess Shaffer states, it is just good to be here in the land of the living. I am so grateful to have life in my body and a mind to think because if I have life in my body, I still have a chance. Despite prevailing conditions, all of God's days are good.

As I look over the years and all the challenges that I have had to deal with, the high points as well as the low points, the joys of victory and the agony of feeling defeat, through it all I have remained steadfast in my faith and maintained my spiritual integrity. I write this book to express my gratitude for my life; it has not always been easy for me.

Being determined to make it as a young father, I didn't know how to make it, but I knew something had to make it work. I didn't always know the Lord, but I take solace in the fact that he knew me. For he carried me during times when I didn't think I would make it, but he did.

Having a nervous breakdown at the age of 21 and feeling so bad about myself because I was on medication and seeing a psychiatrist, my self-esteem plummeted, and I was faced with the issues that precipitated the breakdown. Being estranged from my parents was one thing, but being estranged from myself was even worse. At a critical time in life, I had overextended myself. Working 12-hour shifts in an automobile plant and going to night school as well took its toll on me in a short period of time.

Trying to please everyone else but myself, somewhere I got lost in the shuffle.

My life was falling apart, just too much grief at a time when I didn't know who I was. Trying to hold it together, but I just didn't know how.

On a continuum, when I look back over my life, I know that the Lord has brought me from a mighty long way. He brought me out of the darkness into the marvelous light. To lose your mind and to have it restored not once but twice, I do marvel at that. I am grateful to modern medicine and the medical community. It is easy for me to work in mental health and extend myself to others in a clinical setting for the past 30 years. After all, I am giving back to an entity that I have benefited from.

To put the notion of gratitude in perspective, I will borrow a golden nugget my dad once told me: "I cried because I had no shoes until I met a man who had no feet." Oftentimes, we get consumed with our problems, and we forget our blessings, like the mere fact that we are still here and have life in our body. As David stated: "he once was young but now is old but he has never seen the righteous forsaken or his seed go begging for bread."

The Good Lord is fully aware of what we are capable of and the enormous potential that we have inside of us. As it is stated: "Greater is that which is inside of you than that which is in the world." Although we are limited in the human realm, we have unlimited potential in the Divine mind of Christ. Christ is the mind of God individualized, a consciousness that resides in all of mankind, as Eric Butterworth would say.

God made man from the dust of the ground and formed him in his image and likeness. Then God breathed into the nostrils of man, made a living soul, and infused his spirit into mankind.

Breath and Spirit come from the same root word; essentially the Spirit of the Lord resides within us. Jesus recognized his divinity, and so should we as he stated, the Father and I are one. We should live and exist as if we are in the very presence of God to personalize our relationship with God. To lean on him and not our own understanding and trust in him with all our might.

Forgiveness

To err is human, and to forgive is divine. Forgive me for my trespasses as I forgive those who have trespassed against me. Things happen in life whether we intend for them to happen or not. There is an art to forgiveness. We must move beyond the situation and the corresponding feelings we attach to them, and therein lies the difficulty. Are we ready or willing to let go?

Letting go is as easy to the extent that we allow it to be. Remember the forgiveness is not just for someone else, but it is to liberate you from the self-imposed captivity that we allow ourselves to be in. It is not just what others have done to us but how we internalize those feelings and the subsequent actions we take. WE ARE ALL GUILTY OF THIS. Things happen, but the determinant is our corresponding actions and the choices we ultimately make regarding the matter.

For years, my father and I were at odds with one another. When I look back at that period, I realize those were moments we could not get back. Fortunately, we had a breakthrough and we began communicating again. The breakthrough came at a time when the need to do so was great because a few years later, he died. On reflection, I know God intervened and saw fit that we should reconcile our relationship. We still had a ways to go, but we had closed the gap, and I will be eternally grateful for that.

Not forgiving others prevents you from going to the next level in your Spiritual Awakening because you're holding on to emotions and feelings about an event that has passed, but you continue to live the experience over and over as if it just happened. You are being held captive by your own thinking.

When you forgive, you allow yourself to be free from fears and doubts. You cannot change what has happened, but you can direct the way you enhance or become more fulfilled in your life. The most important thing is that we go through and don't get stuck in gear. We decide which way we are going to go so that we don't get stuck.

Embedded in you are all types of obstacles that prevent your movement. Being consumed with your frustration and contempt for others, you're blinded by rage, and you're stifling yourself. Essentially, like quicksand, the more you struggle, the faster you go down.

So just as you see someone extending a branch to pull you out of the quicksand, it is up to you to receive it. Forgiveness affords you an opportunity to get your life back and to restore you to what you need to be: no longer consumed and directed by your anger toward life, able to appreciate the Christ within you. You can become a new creature in Christ. You can achieve all things through Christ who strengthens you.

Your blessings are blocked when you hold on to resentment and hurt because you transfer that negative energy on to others. You are being conformed to the world when you allow your anger to consume you.

We must be mindful that all through life there is a lesson to be learned, and once we learn it we move on to the next one. Life is a process of continuous improvement. It is not about problems; it is about opportunities to master your circumstances or conditions. If it doesn't kill you, it can only make you stronger.

It's My Time

To everything, there is a season and a time to every purpose under the heaven. Finding your niche in life is the key. Life is full of a lot of twists and turns that seem awkward and cumbersome, but these are the very things that define your being—the ebb and flow, the pains and subsequent gains from them that you didn't anticipate but were there for a purpose. All things work together for good to them that love God, to them who are called according to his purpose.

One must yield to the call and recognize that our experiences in life give a sense of guidance and direction so that God can best use us. We must furnish the life, so God can use us. We must humble ourselves and draw nearer to God. We must allow ourselves to be an instrument of his will.

As I think over my life, I notice that I have spent so much of my time on the interests of others at the expense of myself. I have really neglected my wants and desires, something that was apparent to everyone else but me. I called myself doing the right thing, but I had deprived myself of so much. I spent money and accommodated the needs of others and deferred my own needs like when my daughters were young, and I spent all my money on them as they laughed at my worn-out shoes. A dear friend once told me, "While you're shopping anyway, put something in the buggy for you." I wasn't doing that.

The operative form for me is to accept my divinity and live the life so that God can use me to live as if I am in the very presence of the Lord and to lean on him and not my own understanding and to trust in the process. God knows that our journey will not be easy and that there will be many dangers, toils, and snares that we will have to contend with, but he also knows that we cannot just contend with adversity but to overcome these obstacles. We are endowed with the very attributes of God, so it is incumbent upon us to make full use of them. This is why God expects so much from us. As it is written, we suffer needlessly by allowing ourselves to be separate from God.

As Eric Butterworth stated, Christ is the mind of God individualized, being mindful that to be Christ like is to be God like. It is all about the mind. The Bible is good that way in showing us the mind of Christ by what he spoke of and what he did. God expects so much more out of us than what he is getting. I must rise above the human eclipsiation of life and lean on the divine mind of Christ.

I can do all things through Christ that strengthens me. Although I am limited in the human realm, I have unlimited potential in the divine mind of Christ. I must accept this as a fact and let the process work. I must focus on elevation and agree with God irrespective to the circumstances, for God has decreed the matter, for he will give you the desires of your heart and let his will manifest itself through you. Being mindful that we are the manifestation and expression of God essentially, we are spirits housed in a body. We are more than human beings with spiritual inclinations; to the contrary, our greatest component is our spirituality.

I will spend more time throughout the day acknowledging the Lord and being mindful of his omnipresence that he is in every vacant place and that wherever I am God is also in the midst. I will make a conscious effort to live as if I am I the very presence of God and that my thoughts should agree with him as well. I once heard a song with words that said there is a great change in me. I am so happy I am so free, for he brought me out of the darkness into the marvelous light. Even more so, when God frees you, why should you be bond? I must pursue my assignment and let God work a wonder in my life.

God is my inexhaustible vein of supply, and he can supply my any and every need; all I must do is position myself in the way I think and again let the process work. I am an integral part of God's plan for the salvation of mankind, for he had plans for me when he laid the foundations of this world. For he created mankind in this best of molds with noble intentions a little lower than the angels. As it written, lean on the Lord and not your own understanding and trust in him with all your might, and he will direct your path.

God has a blessing for me. All I must do is reach up in my mind and get it and not allow myself to be separate from God. I must entertain thoughts that are consistent with a Godly persona and reject anything that is contrary to the will of God. As I have been told, the process is likened to a letter that comes to your house that is not yours; you are encouraged to not open and promptly return it to the sender. So, it is with thoughts which are not pleasing to God; we are not to entertain them let them go back into the universe.

The ancient Sanskrit word for man means to think; men are thinkers by nature, which means we should think about what we think about, or as Dr. Lorraine Keefa states, mind your mind. Be careful of the thoughts that we entertain; words have a lot of authority over us.

Our thoughts become self-fulfilling or shall we say prophetic for thoughts are things and words materialized, for as a man thinks in his heart so is he. Therefore, we must agree with God irrespective of the appearance of things. We should not be estranged from one another; that is especially evident in marital relationships. God intended for us to be a helpmate to one another. God created us to be one with one another and that no one and nothing should compromise that union, that we should be twined to one another inseparable.

GOD EXPECTS MORE OUT OF US THAN WHAT HE IS GETTING, FOR HE ORDAINED MARRIAGE AN HONORABLE AND NOBLE INSTITUION THAT HE DESIGNED FOR HIS PURPOSE TO MAGNIFY HIS PRESENCE ON THIS EARTH.

First and foremost, a man and woman are supposed to be twain to each other, and next to God, nothing should get in the way of that bond. Nothing means just that: no third party in any capacity should compromise that relationship. In our case we were instructed to not let any third-party elements be a part or compromise our relationship.

God intended for our marriage to be a sustainable and endearing relationship that could surpass any obstacle; he did not expect a marriage to succumb to what has been so easily ascribed as irreconcilable differences.

We must be mindful that we made a vow to the Lord to conduct ourselves in an honorable manner. **AS IT HAS BEEN STATED, IN GOOD TIMES AND BAD TIMES, AS WELL SICKNESS**

AND HEALTH, AND EVEN MORE SO RICH OR POOR, THAT THE ONLY THING THAT SHOULD SEPARATE YOU IS DEATH.

Well, these days as they say, modern times and modern problems, more than 50 percent of marriages are failing, and just as alarming is those that have not failed are still at risk of failing. My marriage has seen more than its share of challenges. I am tired of this roller-coaster ride that we have been on for far too long.

Sure, it has its high points, but that is offset by its downside. It's not just those elements that are outside of the relationship. Like so many couples, we are challenged by our own inertia, our lack of cohesiveness or unity.

Before her death, Mother Woods asked me, "Do you encourage one another?" Initially, I said yes, but on second thought, I had to say no. Like a lot of couples, we had become complacent and took one another for granted or even more so forgot the value that we had for one another.

The thrill was not necessarily gone in our case, but we felt beaten down by our circumstances. So many things had transpired consistent with the cyclical nature of life—just the vows state the good times and the bad times, the periods of feast (rich) and the times of famine (poor), and periods of good health and periods of illness.

It may sound cliché, but I would rather go through bad times with my wife than good times with someone else. The remarkable thing about our relationship is despite the appearance of things, I still think we have a chance.

If we believe, the best is yet to come. People tend to call me the eternal optimist, and I guess with the experiences that I have had and how God has allowed me to prevail over them, I can afford to be. It is not just what God has done for me, but what he has consistently done for me despite myself.

It is just what I know about the goodness of God and how despite the appearance of things he remains in the blessing business. How God wants us to trust in him and turn to him for guidance and that he wants us to remain steadfast in our faith and to hold on to him despite how things look.

God wants us to look to his faithful servant Job, a man who displayed unwavering faith, a man who displayed spiritual integrity and held on despite the appearance of things. We cannot be consumed with fear and doubt; we must agree with God and let his will be done.

Nowhere is this evident in our relationship with our Lord as evident in our marital relationship. Just as God expects us to be on one accord with him and put nothing before him, in the human realm in our marital relationship, we should be on one accord and our marriage should come first.

I like to borrow a nugget from a dear friend of mine whom I have known since childhood, Florine. She stated, "Calvin, with what I know now about relationships, I would have gotten to know them spiritual before I knew them physically." We must come to know a person in the broadest sense of the term.

To know them is to love them despite the things that impede the process. You should extend yourself to them to bring forth desired results, and they in turn should reciprocate the process. If you are not twinned, you be smart to do so. I am talking about Calvin and Lela right now. The last thing that Lord Shaffer said to us was to draw closer; otherwise, we were going to lose everything. In conjunction with that, he wanted us to be mindful that we were able to do so much better than what we were doing.

Just on that note, the Shaffers had invested a lot into us and our vision to help us on our journey. If there was ever someone who believed in us, it has been the Shaffers. They have been an integral part of our life on many levels, and for that, I will be eternally grateful. They really have been a ram in the bush and have allowed us to circumvent some treacherous waters.

I must be mindful as I write from my change of venue right now as my wife is in the next room taking a nap in our suite at the Peninsula Inn in Niagara Falls. This trip was planned months ago before our separation; I had not planned to be here, but you know what? God intended for me to be here, and I will choose his plans over mine any day of the week.

God has a way of letting his presence not only be known but felt; he has a way of making a way out of no way, of making our crooked way straight.

Now, there are those that say if you are going to leave, then why go back and forth, or is the situation a little bit more complicated than it appears to be? Now our relationship has its complications, but I would never wish harm or misfortune on Lela.

Coming to Niagara Falls by herself was not what she really wanted, and my role as I saw it was to be her escort and all that it entailed. This was a business move; I had to make sure she was all right. Like I said, some things are a little bit more complicated than someone from the outside could see or understand. One cannot go by the appearance of things when it comes to marital relationships, for no one knows what goes on behind closed doors. God in his infinite wisdom takes things which appear to be foolish and confound the wise.

I thank God for being just who he is and doing just what he said he would do. Oh, what a mighty God we serve, who watches over us and has a vested interest in seeing us do well. God wants us to have a full and productive life.

For God not only rules, but he super rules, and he has the final say in all matters; he just wants us to keep his commandments and live in accordance to his will and for us to be an instrument of his will.

It is his desire that we should rise above the human eclipsiation of life and lean on the divine mind of Christ, and Christ is the mind of God individualized. That should be our mantra, that to be Christ like is to be God like, and we can be a new creature in Christ. Our oneness with God should be evident in every facet of our life, our marriage inclusive.

Afterthoughts

After all is said and done, we thought about what we were going to do now. It is often stated that we have identified the problem, and we know that we are messed up. Well just as the problem has been caused by benign neglect on our part, so in large measure the solution does reside within us as well. We did drop the ball, and we were caught up in the hype.

So, let's do something about it. Let's engage in more meaningful dialogue with ourselves and one another. We can start with being our brother's keeper and embracing one another as opposed to recoiling from one another. If there was ever a time to get reacquainted with one another now is the time. This is a time to roll up our sleeves and get the job done.

This sense of rugged individualism does not and has not worked for us. Get our egos and pride out of the way. Stop focusing on the self-imposed limits and look at the possibilities of things happening. For as long as we say that it will not work it will not work. There is an urgent need for radical change in how we view ourselves and the role that we play in our salvation.

Salvation is something that we must initiate and take responsibility for we cannot be passive in our spiritual walk. We cannot defer this to something or someone external to us to achieve our objective. If we only understood the enormous potential that we have inside of us and what we can achieve, we could move mountains.

We must be better acquainted with the true nature that we have and live accordingly. We live in the context of diminished returns when our ultimate reality is to live a full and abundant life. We fall short of the glory of God not because we are inherently deficient, but because we don't strive for excellence because we don't view it as an option. Our contention is that we can't, not that we can.

In the spiritual realm of our existence, we should view ourselves inherently by nature to be one with the creator and to have a spirit-filled existence. That the norm is to walk in the light because we are not held captive by our fears and doubts. Because we recognize that if we can conceive of it as a possibility and believe in it, then it is achievable and within our grasp. The only thing that is holding us back is that we have not considered it as a possibility.

We are and can achieve those things which are the desires of our heart. We look to God for guidance and trust in the process. We have risen above the self-imposed limitations and realize the awesome power that we have as co-creators with the creator. We are at a disadvantage because we have dummied down to fit in. Essentially, we have not because we ask not.

The essence of our existence is defined by the very nature of how we think we must go beyond the traditional assumptions of the way that man defines you and go inwardly to get a clearer definition of who you are. Whether it is within the context of the universal or subconscious mind or the spiritual context of the mind of God or the indwelling spirit, we must go to another level of awareness of who we really are.

The guidance that we get must go beyond the traditional and customary practices which have impeded our journey and adversely impacted the quality of our life. By being constrained in our visionary capacity, it has permeated every facet of our society. It is at the root of marital discord, interpersonal drama, even the rearing of our children.

This disconnection causes us to be estranged from who we are and how we naturally function. We are supposed to be one with the source that we come from. We operate from a vantage point that is contrary to our nature then wonder why we have so many maladaptive tendencies. So, when it is stated that we are not to be conformed to the world but transformed by the renewal of our mind, this tendency is our quest is to realign our thinking with that which is consistent with our true nature.

Again, theses maladaptive tendencies show up in our thinking and our relationships with one another. We are all challenged by the ongoing battle or internal conflict that is going inside of our head and our heart. Then this estrangement shows up in our relationships, and we wonder why we fall and we don't know how to get up. Yes, it is difficult, but there's is also relief, but it comes in the form of another level of thinking.

Yes, we are fortunate to have the resources readily available to us to make our life more manageable and in technical terms to make our life more user friendly. It was not the plan of the creator to be entangled in a way of life that is disorderly because we exist in an orderly universe. So, it is imperative that we form a better relationship with ourselves and one another.

Epilogue: Generational Conflict

As it is written, a generation is born, and a generation dies, but this earth is meant to endure forever. When will we benefit from the errors of our predecessors? When will we get it right? If there was ever a time to resolve this dilemma, now is the time. Haven't we suffered enough?

Knowing that the prayers of the righteous avail much gives me a sense of peace and comfort while going through the difficult times I've faced. One of the last things that Reverend Lord James Shaffer told us was that we had come too far to turn back, that if we didn't draw closer, we were going to lose everything.

You know what? We were on the verge of losing everything again, and we had to take a critical look at ourselves and one another and what this marriage had come to. God expected more out of us than he was getting. This is not the way we started. Our relationship was reconcilable. There was working to do, and we were willing to do the work.

Despite the differences and the difficulties, the relationship was salvageable. We had to move out the way and let the Lord fight our battles and lean on him, being mindful that we serve an awesome God.

We learned the value of not being conformed to the world and that we could be transformed by the renewal of our mind. Our faith was being tested, and we had to rise above the impediments that we were contending with.

The key to our dilemma is that we had to focus more on solutions and not be consumed with our problems. We had to take inventory of ourselves and to approach in a fearless manner. It was when we took a prayerful posture and let God mediate our situation that our life became easier.

Not to oversimplify the process, but we must be more diligent in practicing what we preach if we are to see different results. We can be double-minded and easily uprooted from our faith, but must remain steadfast in our convictions while facing adversity. When we choose to focus on elevating and trusting the process, that is when the renewing of who we are begins. If there was ever a time to personalize our relationship with the Lord, now is the time. We must stop blaming everyone else for our situations and take the time to surrender to the will of God in our lives and transform.

Have we become so disillusioned with the source that we came from? Has the apparatus or institutions that purport to be the Lord's representative maligned our perception of both the representative and the source? Well I know that attendance is down in most places, but we should still attend to our Spiritual needs. We should be one with the creator despite the appearance of things.

For the Lord would never leave us or forsake us; it is mankind that has forsaken the ways of the Lord, and we are suffering immensely. The creator in his infinite mercy is patient with us and gives us ample warning to return to his ways. Like the prodigal son's father, he is waiting patiently, anticipating our return home. He knows that it is not easy for us in the human realm of our existence.

Whatever we wish or desire, it is God's intention that we should have it. Our quest is to be on one accord with God and to operate in a manner that is pleasing to him. Unfortunately, mankind has consistently operated in a manner that is not in agreement with the will of God; consequently, we have brought misery and despair upon ourselves and we have justified our madness. Our errant ways have created an environment that is the antithesis of what the creator has intended for mankind.

Yet still we have not relinquished the hold that this system has on us, and we have consistently allowed ourselves to be led astray by our own devices. One must be mindful that we are to display and convey spiritual integrity regardless of what we are faced with.

We must trust in the process and know that the Lord will put no more on us than what we can bear. There will be mountainous situations that will appear to be insurmountable, but we must trust in the process. We have inherited a mess and the system that we are living under has reached critical mass and it is a mess. But just like we inherited a mess, we also inherited a solution.

For the Lord said that he would raise up a nation that would obey him. He is the same yesterday, today, and tomorrow. He asks that we keep his commandments and live.

IT IS OUR TIME, AND GOD EXPECTS MORE OUT OF US THAN WHAT HE IS GETTING.

WE CAN CHANGE, BUT IT BEGINS WITH THE ACCEPTANCE OF WHO WE CAN BE AND WHO WE ARE IN THE EYESIGHT OF THE CREATOR.

There is a shift in the atmosphere, and a new paradigm is emerging. The former things are going by the wayside. It is time to start expecting more out of ourselves and one another. Mankind must allow the process to work and allow themselves to be a new creature in Christ.

We have suffered long enough in every facet of our being. Marriages have been torn apart, children have run amuck, communities have been in disarray from the top to the bottom, we have lived in a hostile environment, and it has taken its toll on us. Everyone has their story, and we all have the bruises to prove it. We have so much but are underrepresented in the awareness of God. We worship the creation over the creator and act oblivious as to why we suffer.

When we become more aware, we are less likely to be led astray by the illusions of the allure that surround us. Liken to wolves in sheep's clothing, we must pay attention to the subtleties of words that can easily move you emotionally but affect you psychologically.

As Dr. Lorraine Keefa Witherspoon would say, mind your mind and think about what you think about. It is our level of thinking that either makes us or breaks us. The thoughts we entertain have profound implications for the way that we live. We must focus on elevation always and not succumb to our low desires and do that which is pleasing to God first and foremost.

One must master themselves in the world of spirits and acknowledge the need and ability to do so, for we have greatness inside that is to express itself. My wife and I had major challenges that we had to contend with. For 12 years, we battled over the children, finances, and each other's different styles and methodologies. Despite that, we prevailed.

What mattered most for us is that we made a vow to God, and we didn't take it back. We were determined to make it despite ourselves and the appearance of things.

I know it wasn't easy for either one of us, but God took us through it. There was a time when it seemed unlikely, but there were prayer warriors who interceded for us. The teachings of the Universal Triumph the Dominion of God were and continue to be our rock and foundation that we build our marriage on.

Having prayer warriors in our midst that were well versed in the practical side of your spiritual journey. They saw the enormous potential that was inside of us yearning to express itself. Their objective was to aid us and provide the forum for expressing it.

Interesting, I came into the organization wanting to become a minister, and it took the wisdom of the elders to provide me with the opportunities to express myself. The more I talked and expressed myself, the more I wanted to say something. It was like the adage, if I had a thousand tongues I couldn't praise him enough.

I will be eternally grateful for the teachings of the Dominion. It truly was the definitive experience for me. It's nice when someone sees beyond your faults and responds to your needs. People knew that we were a hot mess, but they also understood that we could be salvaged.

These were people that saw through our foolishness and our folly. In a sense, like it is stated, youth is wasted on the young. The congregation was a cross section of a remnant that was just a faithful few, like a lot of churches today.

They understood they needed the youth and the youth needed them, for we need the youth because they are strong, and we need the elders because they know the way. Despite the appearance of things, their goal was to see us through. They were aware that they as well had to transcend their youthful indiscretions. Someone showed them the way, and they were determined to extend that to us as well.

We learned the value of not being conformed to the world and that we could be transformed by the renewal of our mind. Our faith was being tested, and we had to rise above the impediments that we were contending with.

The key to our dilemma was that we had to focus more on solutions and not be consumed with our problems. We had to take inventory of ourselves and to approach life in a fearless manner. It was when we took a prayerful posture and let God mediate our situation that our life became easier.

www.ingramcontent.com/pod-product-compliance
Lightning Source LLC
Chambersburg PA
CBHW061644040426
42446CB00010B/1564

We learned the value of not being conformed to the world and that we could be transformed by the renewal of our mind. Our faith was being tested, and we had to rise above the impediments that we were contending with.

The key to our dilemma was that we had to focus more on solutions and not be consumed with our problems. We had to take inventory of ourselves and to approach life in a fearless manner. It was when we took a prayerful posture and let God mediate our situation that our life became easier.

www.ingramcontent.com/pod-product-compliance
Lightning Source LLC
Chambersburg PA
CBHW061644040426
42446CB00010B/1564